The
Smoked-Foods
Cookbook

The Smoked-Foods Cookbook

❖

How to Flavor, Cure, and Prepare Savory Meats, Game, Fish, Nuts, and Cheese

❖

Lue & Ed Park

STACKPOLE
BOOKS

Copyright © 1992 by Lue Park and Ed Park

Published by
STACKPOLE BOOKS
5067 Ritter Road
Mechanicsburg, PA 17055

Printed in the United States of America

First Edition

10 9 8 7

Published in Canada by special arrangement with Meridian Press,
50 Main Street, Ottawa, Ontario K1S 1B2.   ISBN 1-895771-00-5.

Library of Congress Cataloging-in-Publication Data

Park, Lue
    The smoked-foods cookbook : how to flavor, cure, and prepare
    savory meats, game, fish, nuts, and cheese / Lue Park and Ed Park
    —1st ed.
        p.   cm.
    Includes bibliographical references and index.
    ISBN 0-8117-0116-6
    1. Smoked meat.   2. Smoked fish.   3. Cookery (Smoked foods)
    I. Park, Ed.   II. Title.
    TX609P27   1992
    641.4'6—dc20   92-7047
                                                           CIP

To Tracy, Kelly, and Jeff, who
could consume jerky and smoked fish
faster than we could make it

Contents

Introduction

Smoke-flavored foods command such high prices at markets, delicatessens, and specialty stores that they are often reserved for special occasions. But you can enjoy such foods as smoked salmon, dried jerky, or a smoke-cooked roast anytime you wish once you have learned to make these foods at home with a minimum of space, effort, time, and money. Most types of meats can be smoked, and a smoky flavor can be added to many other foods, including pasta, beans, cheese, and nuts.

Smoking is not an exact science, but it requires experimentation. Such variables as climate and equipment will influence the result. More important, personal tastes vary: what is too sweet or salty for one person will be just right for another.

Smoking foods has a long history. Although we don't know for sure, man probably learned to smoke meats shortly after he discovered fire. We all know from campfire experiences that smoke repels insects. This repellent quality became clear to us when we were on a wilderness pack trip several years ago. We rode horses, while a string of mules carried our gear. At the end of each day, we turned the horses and mules loose to feed on the lush grasses. Then we set up camp, prepared and ate our meals, and gathered around the evening fire.

It was summer, and biting insects swarmed around the livestock, causing them extreme discomfort. We soon noticed that every time we had a fire, two of the mules would walk over and stand with their heads in the heaviest of the smoke. Although the smoke seemed to irritate their noses and eyes, evidently they were less bothered by the smoke than by the insects.

No doubt early man also stood in the smoke of fires to keep insect pests away. Eventually, he may have realized that if smoke kept insects off himself, it would do the same for his meat. Smoking offered another advantage: it also helped in the preservation process. At some point, he must have decided he liked the flavor of smoked meat, too.

Anthropologists speculate that early man did not need salt because he got plenty from the raw meats he ate. When he started cooking meat, however, the salt was leached from the meat, so he had to add salt to his diet. He discovered that salt not only enhances the flavor of foods but also acts as a preservative.

Once he knew how to dry and salt meat, he could preserve it indefinitely. When meat was plentiful, he could dry it and store it for future use; when times were lean, he had a supply of food to sustain him until the next hunt produced more fresh meat.

Until the advent of refrigeration in the late 1870s, salting was the primary method of preserving meats. Smoking played an important part in this curing process. As freezers became more widely used and cooking with wood or coal became less common, the art of smoking foods fell by the wayside. People still loved the flavor of smoked food, however. A new quick-cooking process using charcoal briquettes came into vogue, and soon, most American families had some type of barbecue grill. For additional smoky flavor, hardwood chips were added to the hot briquettes, or liquid smoke flavoring to the marinade or sauce.

The production of fine old-fashioned smoked foods was left largely to the commercial specialty houses. Dry and semidry sausages, ham, bacon, and smoked fish were available only in the deli section of grocery stores or at gourmet food stores.

Of course, a few people such as farmers and avid hunters and anglers, still cured and smoked foods. Yet even these people lacked the space and time required for smoking in traditional smokehouses. Soon, the need for an easier, more economical way to smoke foods was evident.

Companies began to build electric smokehouses, which quickly became popular in many areas of the country. These smokers, or "smoke ovens," as they are called, produce hot-smoked foods such as smoked fish and jerky, and add smoke flavors to many other foods.

Today, smoking foods can be as simple or as sophisticated as you want it to be. Most people use some method of hot-smoking, since it is the quickest and easiest way to add a smoky flavor to a wide variety of foods. Those who have the time and the space may opt for a smokehouse, where meats can be cold-smoked using a more controlled and lengthier process. Regardless of the method, however, we now have the means to produce mouth-watering flavors in smoked foods.

Basic Principles

When we think of smoked meats and other foods, we usually think of flavor first, then preservation. The moister, more lightly salted foods produced today are more palatable than the heavily salted and very dry foods of the past. Remember, however, that heavily salted and dried foods are preserved; today's lightly salted and less dry foods need to be treated as perishable.

There are a number of reasons people choose to smoke foods at home. Doing it yourself is far less costly than buying the finished product. It is a simple, easy process that produces wonderful results. And you can control the salt, sugar, and fat content of your own smoked foods, as well as experiment with herbs and other flavorings.

Advance preparation of food for smoking varies. Cheese and nuts can be smoked without much preparation. Meats and fish are usually marinated or cured before smoking.

Cures are necessary for preserving many kinds of smoked foods, especially meats and fish that are cold-smoked. Salt provides a certain amount of safety in preservation, depending upon how much is used. Although curing salts do not usually have to be added to most meats that are hot-smoked, many people like to add some to the brine or dry cure for the flavor they impart. (See Preparing Foods for Smoking.)

Although the smoke itself does help preserve food, foods are smoked primarily to enhance the flavor. The smoky taste usually comes from hardwoods, each of which gives a slightly different flavor; apple, cherry, maple, hickory, alder, mesquite, and nut woods are good choices. Wood can be used as the heat source itself, or added to another type of heat source to produce just the smoke.

The term *smoking* can be confusing. Sometimes *smoking* means the kind of cold-smoking traditionally done in old rural smokehouses, or it can refer to hot-smoking foods in an electric smokehouse. *Smoking* also applies to smoke-cooking, which is done in a unit designed primarily to slow-cook foods. Some experts differentiate between hot-smoking and smoke-cooking, but others insist smoke-cooking is just part of hot-smoking. Confused? *Smoking* can also mean fast, hot cooking on a barbecue grill, using hardwoods for added flavor. There are other terms used to describe methods of smoking, most of which are hot-smoking. We'll define many of these methods later.

For now, let's clarify the confusion. There are really only two basic types of smoking: cold and hot. Both are based on the same principle: Air is drawn in through openings, usually at the bottom of the smoke chamber (the container in which the food to be smoked is placed). This air swirls around inside and mingles with the smoke, then rises and leaves through openings at the top. While the smoke swirls around the smoke chamber, it penetrates the food. At the same time, the smoke and air pick up moisture from the food and carry it out the top, thereby drying the food.

Sometimes cold-smoking is preferable; other times hot-smoking is better. The choice depends on the foods involved, the equipment available, and the results you desire.

Although there are no official definitions, cold-smoking is generally considered to be at temperatures less than 85 degrees F. Hot-smoking is considered to be at temperatures between 120 and 180 degrees F. The range between 85 and 120 degrees F is considered too warm to be cold-smoking and too cold to be hot-smoking. Expert smokers use this middle range to achieve subtle differences in flavors and textures. Above 180 degrees F you are cooking rather than hot-smoking.

Cold-smoking involves smoking foods under controlled conditions that provide lots of cool smoke. Cold-smoking is used for hams, bacon, some sausages, and some smoked fish.

Here's what you need for cold smoking:

• A way of producing smoke.

- A method for cooling the smoke until it gets to the smoke chamber.
- A smoke chamber in which the meat or fish is smoked.
- Ways to regulate the heat and smoke.

A fire box or pit is most commonly used to burn wood to produce the smoke. A tunnel, trench, or pipe from the fire pit to the smoke chamber is often used to cool the smoke. Many types of containers are suitable as smoke chambers. Temperature controls and drafts are needed on all smoke chambers to regulate the process, which may take two weeks or more.

Cold-smoking dries the food and imparts the smoke flavor but does not actually cook it. This process gives a more pronounced smoke flavor than does hot-smoking because the food is in the smoke for a longer time. Meats are usually cured using curing salts before they are cold-smoked, since the very low heat, moisture from the food, and lengthy processing time can otherwise lead to spoilage. Meats are sometimes cold-smoked, then the temperature is raised and the process finished off with a hot-smoke.

Commercial cold-smoking units can be purchased ready-made or be made to order. You can also construct your own unit for cold-smoking (see Equipment).

Hot-smoking involves smoking foods at higher temperatures, and foods that cook rapidly, such as fish, are usually cooked enough during the hot-smoking process. Many other meats, however, will receive insufficient cooking while being hot-smoked and must be allowed to finish cooking in a hot oven. Much depends on the unit being used, the type of food, and the desired results.

Most people who smoke foods at home use a hot-smoking method. It is not necessary to add curing salts to a brine when hot-smoking at high temperatures, for example, 165 degrees F, since some foods, such as strips of fish, will cook as well as dry at this temperature. Other foods, such as turkey, will not fully cook while in a hot smoker for several hours, but they will be hot enough during this time to be safe before being transferred to a hot oven to finish cooking. Meats become pasteurized when the internal temperature reaches 145 degrees F.

With hot-smoking it is usually not necessary to use curing salts, since the foods reach temperatures hot enough to ensure safety.

Hot-smoking can be done in a wide variety of units:

- Electric smokehouses designed to reach a certain temperature and stay there. Some foods cook at this temperature; others need additional cooking. A pan of hardwood chips over the heat source provides the smoke flavor.

- A typical backyard barbecue unit that usually cooks the food over a high heat. Hardwood chips or chunks on the heat source provide the smoky flavor.
- A barbecue unit with a fire chamber that allows smoke to travel from the fire to a separate smoke chamber. Hardwood logs are the preferred fuel. Foods usually cook slowly, though a hotter fire allows food to cook faster.
- A smoke-cooker that cooks food slowly. Hardwood chunks are used for smoke flavor. A water pan is optional.
- Many other commercial units in a wide variety of designs and price ranges.
- Homemade units in which the temperature is regulated by the unit design, drafts, and amount of fuel used. We describe some of these units in more detail in Equipment.

Hot-smoking is easiest for the home-processor to do, especially in the beginning. For those who are interested in the more complex method of cold-smoking, see the Bibliography.

Keep records in case you want to duplicate something that turned out especially well. Experiment and develop new recipes for your smoked products. In a notebook, record such things as kinds and cuts of food, type of cure and recipe, curing time and drying time, smoking time, heat source, and type of wood for smoke. Make notes on how you thought the product turned out. Did it need more drying time? Was the smoke flavor too strong or too mild? How was the salt content?

We also strongly suggest you experiment after learning the basic principles. How much you experiment will depend on many things, including the equipment and type of wood available, the climate in your area, and your own way of doing things. For example, no two people will build a fire exactly the same way. Much of smoke-cooking is trial and error, or as we like to say, trial and *success*—for if you follow a few basic guidelines, your attempts at smoke-cooking will be successful.

Equipment

As with any project, smoke-cooking requires a certain amount of equipment. The number and kinds of tools you use will depend largely on personal choice. You can rig up some type of container to use as a makeshift smoker, or you may decide to build a smoker that will last for a long time. For many people, buying a commercially made unit is the best option. Other necessities, such as containers for brining or marinating, tongs, and forks, are common items in most kitchens. Let's first explore the most important piece of equipment you'll need: a smoker.

COMMERCIAL SMOKERS

Since manufacturers use different names for different types of units, terminology can be confusing. For example, the same type of unit may be called a smoker, a smoke oven, or a smokehouse. Remember too, that the name alone does not always tell you what a unit will do. Throughout this book we use the words *smoker* or *unit* to describe any kind of equipment that can be used to smoke, smoke-cook, or grill foods.

There are several advantages to purchasing commercial smokers. They are generally easy to use and are available in many sizes and shapes to fit most needs. In addition, commercial smoke-cookers produce a good end product. Most important, they are ready-made.

If you are smoke-cooking for the first time, we strongly suggest using a store-bought unit. Follow the manufacturer's instructions carefully, since each smoker cooks differently. If you're using a home-made unit, you'll have to experiment with cooking times. Smoke-flavoring a pan of ground meat takes much less time than making jerky, and a large roast takes more time than a small roast. A smoker sitting in the hot sun on a dry, calm day will smoke and cook faster than it would on a cold, rainy, windy day. It takes much longer to cold-smoke meat and fish than to hot-smoke them.

There are many brands of commercial smokers. Before buying, find out all you can about the different units, and assess your needs. If one unit does not fit all your needs, you may want to purchase more than one type of smoker.

Regardless of the type, every smoker will have a chamber to hold the food and retain the smoke, and a source of heat and smoke.

Chambers vary greatly in size and shape. The heat can come from any number of sources, including electricity, propane, wood, and charcoal. Smoke is usually produced by some form of wood—for example, sawdust, chips, chunks, and logs.

Basic units have just a chamber and a heat source. Elaborate units have controls such as drafts and baffles, or extra features such as a thermometer, choice of colors, insulation, and attached shelves. The more features a unit has, the more expensive it will be. The more expensive units are often more versatile.

Smoke ovens or smokehouses. These units are usually tall and slender, which permits the smoke to mingle with the air and swirl around the food. Holes at the bottom allow air to enter, and holes at the top enable the air and excess smoke to escape.

The price for smoke ovens or smokehouses varies greatly, depending on the type and size of the unit, which can range anywhere from the smaller models suitable for home use to huge commercial units that take up several floors of a building.

One of the most popular home smokers is the lightweight, comparatively inexpensive electric unit (such as the Little Chief and Big Chief smokehouses manufactured by Luhr Jensen and Sons, or the Totem Food Smokers made by Pop Geer). These units hot-smoke, and may or may not also cook the food, depending on the temperature attained in a particular unit, the weather, and the type of food being smoked. Unlike some other types of units, they are designed primarily to dry foods at fairly hot temperatures.

Electric smokehouses come in several sizes, and can hold about 25 to 100 pounds of food. Some models load from the top, others from the front. The heat source is a hot plate at the bottom of the unit. The smoke is created by a pan of hardwood chips heated on the hot plate.

Small electric smokehouses take up little space and are a good choice for people with a limited area available for smoking foods. Their small size and light weight make them especially popular with campers who have access to electrical hookups.

Smoke-cookers. Like the small electric smokehouses, smoke-cookers are generally tall and slender. Unlike smokehouses, however, smoke-cookers are designed to fully cook the foods. Some of the units in this category include Coleman's Smoker-Grill, Brinkman's smokers, Weber's Smokey Mountain Cooker, and Meco's Water Smokers.

The heat source (gas, electric, or charcoal) is at the bottom of the unit. Wet or dry hardwood chips or chunks are placed on the heat source to create the smoke. If you prefer to cook the food without adding a smoke flavor, simply leave the wood out.

Many units are designed to use an optional water pan, which comes with the unit and sits on a rack above the heat. The water creates humidity in the smoke chamber, helping to prevent food from drying out. The water pan can be filled with plain water, water plus wine, or other liquids and seasonings that will add different flavors during the cooking. The marinade used to prepare the meat or fish can also be added to the water. After the meat is cooked, the liquid in the water pan and the meat drippings can be used as a base for making flavorful gravies and sauces.

The food cooks and smokes on one or more racks above the water pan. Cooking time is normally slow—about twice as long as in a conventional oven.

Although smoke-cookers are primarily designed to slow-cook foods with an optional smoke flavor, they can be used in other ways as well. If you reduce the heat and do not use the water pan, you basically have a smokehouse or smoke oven, which can be used for making jerky or smoked fish. If you remove the top sections, this type of unit can also be used for grilling. Keep in mind, however, that some smoke-cookers don't grill as efficiently as units designed specifically for that purpose.

Of various types of smokers, we probably use the smoke-cooker most often for family meals. Our unit uses propane, so it is quick and simple to use. It is also an appropriate size for our family.

Off-set dual chamber smoker. This smoker does an outstanding job of grilling or barbecuing, slow-cooking, and smoking. It is very popular in the South and is often made at home or in local welding shops. Commercially available off-set dual chamber smokers include the Hondo Smoker, manufactured by the New Braunfels Smoker Company. Many of these steel units are large and heavy and need a permanent location.

The off-set dual chamber smoker basically consists of two cylindrical, horizontal chambers with hinged lids. One chamber is usually larger than the other. The smaller firebox chamber sits below the larger smoke chamber.

Both chambers have fire grates and cooking racks and can be used for grilling. Which chamber you use depends on how much food you want to cook. You can use either chamber separately or both chambers at the same time if more room is needed.

Slow-cooking and smoking are done by using both chambers. The cooking grill is removed from the smaller firebox, and a fire of hardwood logs or chunks is built on the fire grate. This burning hardwood provides both the heat and the smoke. (You can also use briquettes for the heat and wood chunks for smoke.) When the fire dies down, the food is placed in the larger smoke chamber, which has one or more sets of cooking grates.

A unit with a thermometer, draft, and adjustable dampers on the door and on the smokestack makes it easy to control the heat. You can cook the food by either the long, slow method (at 250 to 300 degrees F) or the quick method, in a conventional oven at 350 to 375 degrees F.

Barbecue grills. Barbecue grills are usually horizontal or spherical, though they can also be round, oblong, or square. Years ago, charcoal was the heat source for most barbecue grills. Charcoal grills are still popular but many units are now electric or gas.

Basic units simply grill the food over high heat; more sophisticated grills have lids and temperature controls that allow slow-cooking. Many features and accessories are available.

The food is usually cooked over high heat, using wood chips or chunks to produce smoke flavor, if desired. In a typical unit, a rack above the heat source holds lava rock or ceramic rock, which distributes the heat. Above that is a pan for catching drippings, then the grill on which the food is placed. A lid covers the entire cooking surface.

Barbecue grills range from small tabletop designs for picnic use to the large, deluxe wagon-style grills. One of the most enduring models over the years has been the kettle-type grill. It is basically a sphere cut in half horizontally. The bottom half holds the heat source, the cooking grate is set on top of that, and the top half of the sphere is the lid.

The larger top-of-the-line units have hinged domed lids. The more expensive units have many controls and accessories.

Among the widely distributed brands are Arkla, Sunbeam, and Weber.

Other commercial smokers. There are many types of units on the market that don't fit in the above categories. One is the Oriental version, which can be made of a variety of materials, including clay, metal, brick, or stone. These smokers are sometimes found in stores that carry barbecue units. They are usually egg-shaped, with a flat bottom, and have a draft door and a smoke vent with controls. The firebox is at the bottom, with cooking racks above. The food can be placed on or hung from these racks. The Oriental-type smokers are designed to be used with a lid, as a smoker or smoke-cooker.

Another model on the market is the portable barbecue unit manufactured by the Pyramid Company. This unit is lightweight and compact and can be used as an oven, stove, roaster, or smoker. Specially designed grates enable you to cook hamburgers and hot dogs over moderate temperatures, or to reach very high, fast temperatures for sautéing, roasting, or broiling, all with just a few charcoal briquettes. Wood chips, Sterno, or other solid fuels can also be used. The units are stainless steel, so they are durable and easy to clean. There are many portable folding models for use in the car or boat, and some permanent standing models for home use.

Another design that quickly cooks and smokes food is the Kiwi Oven. It is a small, portable metal box that uses denatured alcohol or Sterno as a heat source. Wood chips provide a smoke flavor.

Some units are sold only in certain regions of the country, so look around and see what is available in your area.

For those who are more serious about smoking foods, there are many insulated commercial smokers with various controls to suit individual needs. The more elaborate models are available only from butcher supply or specialty stores that carry commercial equipment.

COMPARING THE MODELS

Before purchasing a smokehouse, smoke-cooker, off-set dual chamber smoker, or barbecue grill, you should consider the following:

Use. What type of smoke-cooking do you think you will do the most?

Size. What type of unit do you have room for? The apartment dweller probably can't accommodate a 165-pound off-set dual chamber smoker, or even one of the larger barbecue grills, but he would most likely have room for a small electric smokehouse, or a smaller barbecue grill. The homeowner has many more options.

Cost. Prices range from a few dollars on up. Lower-priced units do the basics; more expensive units are most versatile.

Location. Where will the unit be used? Will you need to move it around? Will it be out of the wind and protected from the elements? Do you want it easily accessible from a kitchen or back door? Consider traffic patterns and safety, especially if you or your neighbors have small children or pets. Some units become very hot during use, so they should be kept away from anything combustible, including the sides of the house or wooden fences. Others will tip over easily during a strong wind or when bumped.

Heat source. Are you looking for an electric, gas, charcoal, or wood-burning unit? Is hardwood readily available and inexpensive? Smoke-cooking could become expensive if you live in the city and have a unit that requires hardwood logs.

Convenience. Can you easily add more fuel, wood for smoke, and water to the water pan? Is it easy to insert or remove food?

Cleanup. Most units require little cleaning other than washing the grill racks and water pans. Stainless steel is less trouble to clean but more expensive.

Storage. In some parts of the country, smokers can sit outside year-round. (If the unit is stored outside, it is a good idea to keep it covered.) In other areas, they must be moved into a shed or under the carport for winter use, or put away entirely. Not all units are easy to pick up and transport.

(For a list of selected manufacturers of the different types of units mentioned above, see Sources at the back of this book.)

HOMEMADE SMOKERS

Some people prefer to make their own smokers. You may want a very simple device for experimenting with smoking foods before you invest in a more expensive model. Or you may do a lot of home smoking and may want to build a unit to your personal specifications. Cost may be another factor.

There are many variables to consider when building your own unit—for example, how much space you have available and what type of smoking you plan to do.

The homemade smoker can be as simple or as grandiose as you wish and can be constructed of almost anything that will hold smoke and food. The simplest smoker we've seen resembled an Indian tepee. While Ed was on a hunting trip with friends, one of the hunters shot a deer the first day. The weather was hot, so they decided to make jerky. They constructed a tepee of poles and a tarp and built meat-drying racks inside from more poles. Then they brined strips of deer meat overnight and laid them across the racks inside the tepee. Finally, they built a smudge fire on the ground beneath the racks. At the end of the hunt, they all enjoyed a tasty jerky.

Fishermen sometimes build makeshift smokers out of cardboard or wooden boxes for whipping up a batch of fresh, hot smoked fish. (Keep in mind that temporary smokers are just that, and remember the hazards of fire.) You can also use wood or steel barrels as smokers. Wooden ones are easier to cut and modify, but the staves eventually shrink from the heat, leaving large gaps that allow too much smoke to escape. Fifty-gallon steel barrels or drums are more difficult to cut and work on, but they last much longer and don't crack. With either type of barrel, you will have to modify or completely remove the tops and sometimes the bottoms. You will also have to devise a way for smoke to enter the chamber at the bottom and exit near the top. In addition, there must be a way to get the food into the chamber.

Many people adapt old refrigerators and upright freezers for use as smokers. These boxes have built-in racks and are already insulated, and the doors make loading and unloading food convenient.

Another alternative is to construct a smoker from wood, bricks, stone, or building blocks. You can build one to whatever scale fits your needs.

In the 18th and 19th centuries, smokehouses were commonly used for curing, as well as for storing meat and fish. Many of these early smokehouses were almost airtight, though it was essential that the smoke be vented properly through either vent holes or a chimney. For both safety and insulation, most of the structures were con-structed largely of nonflammable stones or bricks rather than wood. The fire was usually built inside the smokehouse, in a pit, or in a fire-place. Sometimes it was built outside in a special structure, and the smoke was channeled into the main smokehouse.

Regardless of the type of homemade smoker you choose, every unit must have a chamber to hold the food and detain the smoke, as well as a source of heat and smoke. The smoke and heat come from hardwood logs, chips, chunks, or sawdust; charcoal briquettes, with hardwood added to produce smoke; or a gas burner or electric heating element under a pan of wood chips or sawdust.

The smoke chamber is usually built vertically. Although the smoke must be contained, it must also circulate around and up through the smoke chamber and out the top. In some homemade smokers there are enough cracks and other openings to allow for air circulation. In tightly constructed smokers, such as those made from refrigerators or steel drums, however, holes must be cut at both the top and the bottom. It helps if these holes (called drafts) are adjustable to some degree; that way you can control the air flow, which in turn controls the heat, smoke, and moisture.

Baffles disperse smoke through the smoke chamber and are an optional feature. If you find that smoke distribution is not even, you may want to consider installing a baffle.

All smokers need racks and hooks to put the food on. Old refrigerators and freezers usually come equipped with racks. For other homemade smokers, metal racks can be obtained from various sources, such as old refrigerators, freezers, barbecue grills, or ovens, or they can be cut from metal screening. You can also make racks from metal or wood. Hooks can easily be made from stiff wire. If you use dowels or other round rods, make the ends square or cut a V so that they won't turn around in the brackets when food is placed on them. Do not use racks that are galvanized or cadmium-coated, because they can be toxic. Wooden dowels work well for racks, but they must not be painted or varnished.

Be careful not to place the racks too close together; to smoke properly, the pieces of food must not touch each other. Leave about eight inches above the top rack to allow moisture to gather before it goes out the top vents.

In addition to racks and hooks, you will need a drip pan so that grease doesn't fall into the fire pit and cause flare-ups. You can use an actual pan or simply a sheet of aluminum foil. Sometimes such a drip pan can also act as a baffle.

To keep track of the temperature in the smoke chamber, you can install a thermometer on the outside of the smoker. Cut a hole in the middle of the smoke chamber, then insert the long probe.

Steel drum smoker. Many people find it convenient to construct a smoker from a fifty-gallon steel drum. Be sure to clean the drum to avoid any possible contamination. Cut out the top end of the drum. Then, at the bottom, cut a side door big enough to allow for the firebox. The door should be hinged and have a latch in it so that you can keep it closed. The door also serves as a draft.

You can make racks to hold the food by cutting circles from a steel screen to fit the drum. If you search secondhand or junk stores, you might find old barbecue grills that fit inside the steel drum. The racks should have strong handles, since they will be lifted in and out of the drum.

To secure the racks, you can drill holes and insert bolts. If you prefer, you can push metal or wooden rods through the holes to support the racks.

As an alternative to racks, you can place a piece of steel screen across the top of the drum, then another container such as a box or washtub (with vents cut in the top) over the top of the food.

To improve smoke circulation, try making a baffle from a smaller circle of metal and install it in the lower half of the drum.

For a heat source, you can use an electric hot plate, along with a pan of wood chips to provide the smoke. You can also place briquettes or wood in a pan or bucket. Or, you can dig a fire pit beneath the drum.

Dig the fire pit about 2 to 2½ feet deep and just slightly smaller in diameter than the drum. Line the pit with rocks, or set a metal box down inside the pit. Then position the drum over the fire pit and support it with cement blocks, bricks, or metal strips or bars. If you prefer, you can build the fire on the ground and use bricks or other non-flammable materials to support the smoke chamber above.

Converted refrigerator smoker. An old refrigerator shell, with the motor removed, can often be obtained for free. Look for models that do not have a freezer unit at the top or bottom, and that have one single large door rather than double doors.

Since refrigerators are insulated, the interior of the smoker remains at a more uniform temperature. In addition, the outside of the unit does not get hot.

Refrigerators already have a few built-in racks, and you can always add others, if necessary. The door allows easy access for loading and unloading food in the smoker.

For adequate air and smoke flow, be sure the refrigerator shell has vents. Sometimes there are enough openings if the motor and refrigeration coils have been removed. Otherwise, you will need to cut openings. One way is to cut a hole 6 to 8 inches in diameter in the top. To regulate the flow of smoke, this hole should have a cover that can be adjusted. Or, buy a 3-foot smokestack with a damper, 6 or 8 inches in diameter, then cut a round hole to fit the pipe you bought. Cut several smaller holes into the sides of the refrigerator, near the bottom, for draft.

The heat source is frequently a hot plate placed at the bottom of the refrigerator. Fill a pan with hardwood chips for smoke and set it on the hot plate. You can use an old cast iron skillet or a stainless steel pan. Remember that cast iron does rust. Stainless steel, on the other hand, will remain free of rust and other stains.

Another way to provide a heat source is to cut away the bottom of the refrigerator and place the refrigerator over a fire pit, as described above for the steel drum smoker.

Warning: Since small children like to hide and play in old refrigerators, it is important to keep the smoker locked when you aren't using it.

Wood, masonry, or stone smoker. Most of us do not have the space or the need for the large, elaborate smokehouses that were a part of most farms and ranches years ago. Nevertheless, a scaled-down model, made from traditional materials, is a suitable option for today's smoke-cookers.

For a walk-in model, you may want to consider dimensions of at least 6 feet square by 6 feet high. If the smoker is built of wood, you can line the inner walls with tin or aluminum to help reflect heat.

If you are interested in building a replica of the large smokehouses, check your local library for books that give detailed dimensions and instructions. Or, use the instructions as guidelines to come up with your own design.

It helps to have some knowledge of masonry if you want to build a brick or stone smoker. These smokers are built to last, and when well constructed, have a more pleasing appearance than many other types. They are constructed like a chimney, with the fire chamber at the bottom and a door to cover it. The door can also act as a draft. If the door slides, you can adjust the draft more easily. Directly above the firebox is the baffle. Above that is the smoke chamber, which holds several racks for the food. Holes at the top allow excess smoke to escape.

Adjustments for cold-smoking. A heat source placed directly under the smoker produces too much heat to cold-smoke foods. If you want to cold-smoke meat and fish in your homemade smoker, you will need a fire pit or firebox, a smoke chamber in which the food is smoked, not cooked, and a smoke tunnel that takes the smoke from the fire pit to the smoke chamber. The fire chamber, whether a pit or some kind of container, must be placed lower than the smoke chamber and at least several feet away from it. A tunnel of some type then channels the smoke from the fire pit to the smoke chamber, and cools the smoke before it arrives at the smoke chamber. This tunnel can be a trench covered with wood, metal, or cardboard with perhaps a layer of dirt on top. You can also use a large pipe buried or placed on top of the ground for the smoke tunnel. A piece of stovepipe or large PVC pipe is suitable to channel the smoke.

SMOKER MAINTENANCE

Smokers require little maintenance beyond keeping the racks and water pan clean, and occasionally wiping other parts of the unit after they have cooled. To clean the racks, use a stiff barbecue grill brush, then soak in hot water and ammonia. You will also need to wash the water pan after each use. Try lining it with foil beforehand to make cleanup easier. If necessary, wipe off the drip pan or soak it in sudsy water. Keep in mind that grills and pans are easier to clean soon after they have cooled. Rinse everything well after using cleaners.

Keeping the grills and water pans clean helps prevent deposits from building up and mixing with the food, which can cause a bitter taste. Cleaning the grills and pans regularly also keeps rodent and insect problems to a minimum. In fact, if mice are a problem where you live, it is a good idea to keep both the grills and water pans covered, since mice have a way of getting into places they aren't wanted.

HEAT AND SMOKE

Smokers, whether commercial or homemade, use various kinds of fuels. The most common are charcoal, electricity, gas, and wood. Some units are designed to use only one type of fuel; others are more flexible. In some cases, wood is both the heat source and the source of smoke. Smokers that do not burn wood for heat use hardwood sawdust, chips, or chunks for smoke.

Charcoal briquettes are widely available, relatively inexpensive, and burn hot. They are also easy to transport, and thus are perfect for picnics and camping trips. They can even be used in a pan or on the ground. On the other hand, briquettes are messy and bulky. Be sure to keep them dry; if briquettes get wet, they won't burn as well, even if they have been dried out.

Most people don't know that charcoal briquettes are composed of more than just charcoal. They are usually made from a variety of combustible substances pressed together. Some manufacturers use a combination of hardwood and softwood for the carbon, plus a starch binder. Other briquettes are made from such diverse woods as mesquite, olive wood, or old whiskey barrels.

The better charcoal briquettes are made from quality wood products. Cheap briquettes are made of anything from floor sweepings to petroleum-based products. You should choose high-quality briquettes even if it means paying a little more. A cheaper brand may not burn as hot or as long and may give an unpleasant flavor to the food.

Lump charcoal may also be used as fuel for smokers. It produces a hotter fire and stays hot longer than charcoal briquettes, and it also adds a pleasant odor to cooked food. Lump charcoal is expensive and difficult to find, however.

Getting charcoal lit takes a little more effort than just lighting a match to it. Backyard barbecuers who use lighter fluid pile the charcoal together in the center of the unit, squirt on lighter fluid, touch off a match, then stand back to avoid singed hair. With lighter fluid, it usually takes about half an hour for the charcoal to be ready for cooking.

If an electrical outlet is available, try using an electric starter to get the charcoal started. Electric starters are safer because there is no flare-up (as there can be when lighter fluid is used), and they are inexpensive to use. The charcoal also gets started a little faster than with lighter fluid.

Another device for getting briquettes started is a small metal chimney shaped much like the old campfire coffeepot. The bottom has vent holes, and a rack just above that holds the briquettes. The unit creates a vigorous draft which gets the briquettes going quickly. Other fire starters include small compressed cakes or cubes of various materials, such as sawdust and wax. These are especially handy when camping or picnicking.

Never use kerosene, gasoline, or other flammable liquids to start the fire. Not only are they dangerous, but they will also impart their unpleasant flavor to the food.

Electricity is an excellent heat source because it is fast, clean, safe, inexpensive, and convenient to use. The only major disadvantage is that you must have an electrical hookup. Hardwood chips and chunks are used for smoke flavor.

Gas smokers that use propane or butane are clean and hot, burn even faster than electricity, and are often portable. Some units are designed to be hooked up to natural gas lines.

Wood is still a very common heat source, especially for the large homemade smokehouses and some of the commercial units, such as the off-set dual chamber smokers. Wood is used as a source of smoke in all types of units.

There are at least two disadvantages to wood: it can be difficult to obtain in some areas, and after cooking you have to remove ashes from the firebox. Nevertheless, many people find wood to be the best option as a heat source.

For fuel or smoke, you should use only hardwoods, such as hickory, apple, cherry, pear, beech, chestnut, maple, or oak. As a general rule, stay away from softwoods, such as fir, pine, and cedar, which will give off sooty smoke and produce a dark product with a bitter flavor. Softwoods will also leave a sticky, resinous coating on the inside of the smoker.

Other woods used for smoking include mesquite, alder, mountain mahogany, the nut woods, grapevine, olive wood, palmetto, and mangrove. Dry corncobs are used in some areas, and there are wood chips made from whiskey barrels. For a special touch, there are also small boxes of different woods, such as basil wood, that you can add to the heat source. Or you can soak dried herbs and put them on the heat source.

When used as a heat source, wood is usually burned in the form of small logs or larger chunks. When used as a source for smoke, wood can be in the form of sawdust, chips, or chunks, which are placed on other heat sources to produce the desired smoke. Keep in mind that wood chunks give off a stronger smoke flavor than do briquettes made of wood. Wood can be used dry or wet, depending on the unit and how the food is being smoked and cooked. In some units, such as the small electric smokehouses or smoke ovens, the smoke comes from dry hardwood chips; other smokers are designed to use damp sawdust or soaked chips or chunks.

The most economical source of wood depends on where you live. In the Pacific Northwest, for example, alder is very common, and residents can often cut their own. Other woods, such as mesquite, must be shipped in. On the other hand, mesquite is common in the Southwest. If you travel, you might consider bringing hardwoods home with you. We live in central Oregon, where hardwood is not readily available, so when we travel over the mountain to the valley, we sometimes bring back hardwood to use in our smoker.

Hardwood chips and chunks are available at some supermarkets, cookware shops, hardware stores, and outdoor sports shops, and from a few outdoor supply catalogs. Wood can also be ordered directly from some manufacturers. If you own a unit that burns small logs for fuel and smoke, you can cut and dry your own, or you can buy it from wood cutters.

Some expert smokers use green wood; others advise against it. Green wood produces more smoke, so it is adequate for quick smoking. It is probably not a good idea to use green wood for long-term smoking, however, since the smoke flavor could become too strong.

We learned the value of green twigs and leaves for quick smoke flavoring while on a float-fishing trip. For our shore lunches, we kept a few fish that we had caught each morning. Our boatmen built a charcoal briquette fire under a grill, then added bunches of green alder twigs and leaves. Then they placed the filleted fish on the grill in the heavy smoke. The alder quickly burned up, and the fish was cooked with heat from the charcoal. As a result, the fish had just the right amount of smoke flavor.

Feel free to experiment with different woods, including green wood, for smoke-cooking. Try small batches of food until you are more confident about the results.

OTHER EQUIPMENT

Knives are essential to smoke-cooking. To make the job of cutting meat and fish easier, keep knives sharp. Despite what some people may think, sharp knives are also safer than dull ones. Keep a knife sharpener handy and use it often. You can sharpen knives with a steel, a stone, or a ceramic sharpener, or with one of the many gadgets on the market. We usually use a steel or a stone, depending on the knife.

Stainless steel knives are popular and advertised as staying sharp a long time. When they become dull, however, it may take a professional knife sharpener to put a good edge back on them. Carbon steel is a good, economical choice. Knives of carbon steel may dull fairly easily, but you can sharpen them with a few quick strokes across a steel. The disadvantages of carbon steel are that some foods discolor it, and it will rust easily. But a few rubs with steel wool quickly restores the shine on carbon steel knives.

As an investment, consider purchasing knives of high carbon stainless steel; they are fairly easy to sharpen and do not tarnish and rust. The initial cost may seem prohibitive, but remember that high-quality knives will last a lifetime. Besides, it is frustrating to try to cut meat and fish with poor-quality, dull knives. On the other hand, using a good sharp knife is a joy.

On a trip one winter, we stopped to visit some people who had just gotten a deer and were boning it out. Not only was this their first attempt at boning out big game, but they were trying to do it with dull knives. The result: a lot of extra work on their part, and a lot of hacked-up chunks of meat.

There are many brands of knives from which to choose, and your preference may be different from ours. We suggest selecting from a known brand and a reputable dealer. Whatever your choice, you will need at least three knives: a fillet knife to fillet fish, a carving knife to cut and slice large pieces of meat, and a smaller slicing knife to slice meat for jerky and other purposes.

In addition to knives, you will need containers in which to brine and marinate meat and fish. At least one of these should be large enough to totally submerge turkeys and other large pieces of meat in a brine or marinade. These containers should be made of crockery, glass, plastic, or stainless steel (but no other metal). You should also have covers for the containers, though often foil or plastic or old plastic lids are adequate. For the large crock, we have found that a large plate or round platter, weighed down, works well to keep the meat submerged in the brine or marinade.

An instant-read thermometer is important for checking sausages and meats. These are different from standard meat thermometers because, as the name implies, they read the temperature instantly. Keep in mind, however, that in order to get a correct reading, the food must be at least an inch thick. A thermometer is the only sure way to test for doneness, which is especially important with pork and bear. You will also find good use for a meat thermometer with a long probe; it is either inserted into the meat inside the smoker or put through the hole in the smoker and pushed into the meat.

Several miscellaneous kitchen items that are helpful in smoke-cooking include spoons, tongs, and spatulas. Wood and stainless steel spoons are good for stirring, dipping, and basting. Tongs are helpful in removing the meat from the brine and in handling sausages, as well as for handling hot meat in a smoker. Look for the spring-loaded style. Spatulas are needed for lifting and turning. Select one with a long, broad blade; the handle should be offset from the blade. Using two spatulas at the same time when picking up large fish or fillets helps keep the fish from breaking up.

A fork with sharp tines can be used to pierce meat before it is marinated, to help the marinade penetrate the meat. Long-handled forks are useful for working over hot grills.

For kitchen implements, go to a professional kitchen supply house. The standard household versions tend to be a bit flimsy; the sturdier ones, though more expensive, will do a better job and last longer.

Long-handled basting brushes come in handy when adding a basting sauce or marinade or a last-minute glaze to the smoking meat. Hinged, wire mesh grills are good to have on hand for small or delicate foods. A spray such as Pam is useful for oiling the cooking racks. When you are handling hot items, a pair of mitts or gloves will prevent burns. Wire or nylon brushes help keep cooking racks clean.

An important item for any kitchen is a nonporous, hard plastic cutting board. Wood cutting boards are not safe for cutting up chicken, pork, or bear since they cannot be easily cleaned or sterilized. The plastic boards are not only easy to clean, but also lightweight.

Although a kitchen scale isn't necessary, it comes in handy when measuring out ingredients by ounces and pounds. Some recipes, especially those for sausages, call for ingredients measured by weight. A scale takes away the guesswork. An inexpensive model is perfectly adequate for this type of measuring.

A salinometer, which measures salt content in brines, is also optional. You'll find it useful if you like to make your own brines and want to be exact about salt content, or if you use brines more than once and want to see how diluted they have become.

Heavy-duty aluminum foil is used to wrap foods for storing in the refrigerator, or for freezing. Both sheet foil and foil pans are useful in smoking small items, such as pasta, nuts, and beans; perforate the bottom to allow the smoke to envelop the food. Plastic wrap and plastic bags, depending on their size and thickness, can be used to store food in the refrigerator or freezer. They are also convenient for marinating smaller cuts of meats and fish.

As you cure, marinate, and smoke various foods, you'll discover other equipment that is helpful, too.

We suggest that you start out with a comparatively inexpensive smoker, make small batches of smoked meat and fish, and then go from there.

Safety and Health

Good care at all stages of preparation determines both the quality and safety of the meals later on. Domestic meat, until it is purchased at the market, is subject to government inspection, but care of game and fish is the responsibility of the hunters and fishermen themselves. Although much depends on the situation, game and fish should be dressed as soon as possible and kept clean, cool, and dry.

From here on, the basic care of all meat and fish is the same. Whether it is beef or chicken purchased in a market, or wild game or fish you've harvested yourself, it may be kept for a short period of time in the refrigerator. For long-term storage, however, meat or fish must be canned, frozen, or otherwise preserved.

GENERAL COOKING AND SMOKING

Most meat or fish, whether domestic or wild, can be prepared by most methods.

It is difficult to give specific times for smoking and smoke-cooking foods, since there are so many variables. Smoking time is determined by the kind and size of the food and weather, the type of smoking being done, and the type of unit being used. Refer to the table Approximate Smoke-cooking Times at the back of this book.

To determine when food is done, use a meat thermometer whenever possible. It is a good idea to have two kinds: one that is inserted into the meat and stays there during cooking time, and an instant-read thermometer that registers immediately when stuck into the meat or sausage. Check the food when the minimum cooking time is up, and go from there.

We strongly suggest you keep records as you go along. Jotting down what you did and what you think of the results will help you greatly the next time.

Safety and health are important to consider anytime you are handling animal products, preparing foods, or using smokers where there is a possibility of burns or fire.

DISEASES

Although the odds of getting a disease from handling wild animals are small, they should not be discounted. The most common disease of this type, tularemia, can be contracted from rabbits, squirrels, and other animals.

Tularemia is caused by the bacterium *Pasteurella tularensis,* which is carried by ticks, fleas, and lice. Although it is found in many animals, cottontails are the worst offenders. Cottontails are the most widely hunted and eaten of all game animals, so both the hunter and the cook need to know what to do. If you hunt, always use plastic or rubber gloves when dressing animals. Since the organism can pass through human skin, it pays to be extra careful when handling an infected animal. Small white spots on the animal's liver are one sign of tularemia, but if you don't wear gloves, you may already be contaminated by the time you discover the rabbit has tularemia. When finished dressing the animal, wash your hands, gloves, and knives with hot, soapy water. Freezing the meat does not kill the bacteria, but thorough cooking will.

Some diseases can be contracted by eating improperly cooked foods. Trichinosis is perhaps the most widely known of these diseases and is caused by eating the undercooked meat of domestic hogs, wild boars, and bears, as well as some marine animals, such as walrus, some seals, and the beluga whale. Domestic hogs are particularly susceptible, depending on their feed.

Trichinosis is caused by small worms (trichinae) that burrow in the muscles. The worms enter the human body when a person ingests infected meat. The digestive process frees the larvae, which then attach themselves to the lining of the lower intestine. As they mature, they are carried to the lymph nodes, heart, lungs, and brain, and throughout the rest of the body. Symptoms may appear in two to nine weeks, and each stage produces a separate set of symptoms. Acute cases can sometimes be misdiagnosed as the flu or a virus.

To avoid contracting the disease, always fully cook pork, bear, and other susceptible meats—until the internal temperature reaches 185 degrees F. *Never* eat raw or pink pork or bear. If, when making sausage, you wish to correct the seasoning, cook a small amount of the mixture before tasting it.

The trichinae can also be killed by freezing. If you choose to freeze the meat, follow the U.S.D.A. regulations: -20 degrees F for 6 to 12 days, -10 degrees F for 10 to 20 days, or -5 degrees F for 20 to 30 days. (You can also buy certified pork that has been frozen according to U.S.D.A. regulations and comes with a tag attached.) The arctic strain of the disease can survive long periods of subzero temperatures, so be especially careful if you eat bear from northern climates.

FOOD POISONING

Proper food handling is very important in helping to prevent food poisoning. Such factors as cleanliness, proper cooking times, and proper canning procedures are all vital and help keep harmful bacteria from thriving in meats and some vegetables.

Although botulism is the least common type of food poisoning, it is the deadliest. Botulism attacks the respiratory system; symptoms begin eight to seventy-two hours after poisoning. Since the symptoms appear only after the contaminated food is thoroughly ingested into the body, the poisoning is often fatal.

Knowledge of botulism is important when smoking meat and fish, especially when cold-smoking foods like sausage. The moist food goes into a dark smoker with low temperatures, and the heat and smoke remove oxygen. This can be an ideal situation for the botulism spores to begin producing poison.

Botulism is caused by the spore-forming bacterium *Clostridium botulinum*. Botulism spores are found in every type of meat and vegetable, in the soil, and in water. Although the microbe itself is harmless, it produces one of the most poisonous substances known. According to a 1976 news release from the Health Protection Branch of Health and Welfare Canada, it is estimated that one cupful of the pure toxin could kill the entire population of the world.

The toxin is a by-product of the microbe's germination process and grows only under anaerobic conditions; it cannot multiply in the presence of oxygen. The spores thrive when a combination of factors are present, including low acidity, lack of oxygen, moisture, proper nutrients, and temperatures between 40 and 140 degrees F. The spores can be killed only by pushing the heat up to at least 240 degrees F, but the botulism toxins can easily be destroyed if food is boiled for at least ten minutes.

Salmonella is the most common cause of food poisoning. This genus of bacteria comprises approximately 200 organisms, which are found in poultry, eggs, fish, and raw meat, as well as in contaminated water. Once the food is contaminated, the bacteria grow at a rapid rate. To ensure safety, handle food carefully and make sure internal meat temperatures reach at least 160 degrees F. Unfortunately, there is no way to identify tainted foods by their odor. Eight to seventy-two hours after poisoning, symptoms of pain, diarrhea, nausea, and vomiting will appear. Since salmonella is an infection, antibiotics are an effective cure.

Staphylococcus, or staph bacteria, produces a toxin in foods such as meats and poultry. Unfortunately, as with salmonella, there is no way to tell tainted foods by their odor. Almost immediately after consuming the contaminated food, the victim becomes violently ill with vomiting, nausea, and cramps. The illness lasts about twenty-four to forty-eight hours. Antibiotics are not effective.

If the toxin produced by staphylococcus is already present in the food, heat will not destroy it. Unlike other microorganisms, staphylococcus can also withstand high concentrations of sugar and salt. The best way to prevent this type of poisoning is to refrigerate all meats, even in winter. Also, be sure to clean up the cutting area and utensils after working with any meat. Wooden cutting boards are a hazard because they are difficult to clean and sterilize. The new hard plastic boards work well, since they are nonporous and easily cleaned.

FIRE HAZARDS

Anytime you are dealing with fire or fire-related equipment, you should consider safety. For example, some smokers are not as sturdy as others, and tip over easily. Many get hot enough to burn children, pets, or careless adults.

On a fishing trip to Canada, Ed witnessed the dangers of smoke-cooking firsthand. An employee of the lodge where he was staying rigged a temporary smokehouse of poles and tarps, then built a fire on the ground in the center of this makeshift building to provide the smoke. The results were predictable: the whole thing burned down.

Fortunately, nothing else caught fire. (Interesting enough, the walleye fillets were smoke-cooked to perfection.) In other situations, a fire from a smoker could have serious consequences. Regardless of the type of unit you are using, there must be sufficient heat to create smoke. Always keep in mind the amount of heat being produced, and the distance of the smoker from anything flammable.

All of the above is meant to inform, not intimidate. Use common sense and exercise reasonable care.

Preparing Foods
for Smoking

Most foods are treated in some manner before they are smoked. This treatment may be as simple as sprinkling on some salt, or it may involve soaking the meat for many days in a brine or marinade composed of many ingredients.

INGREDIENTS

The primary components of dry cures and brines are salt and sugar. There are many kinds of salts and sweeteners; in some cases, it doesn't matter which is used, but in other cases it does. In addition, many other ingredients can be used to enhance the finished product.

As long as you follow certain rules for safety and guidelines for good flavor, we encourage you to experiment. Begin by following the recipes in this book, then consider using some of the ingredients listed below to find combinations you prefer. One person will like more or less salt than another. Some people are especially fond of garlic or pepper; others don't like or can't eat either. Adjust recipes to fit your individual tastes.

Salt. All animals must have a certain amount of salt in their diet to survive. Early man ate raw meat, which provided him with plenty of salt. Later, when he learned how to cook meats in water, the natural salt was lost in the process, so he began searching for other sources of salt. He found it by burning certain plants, then later, by actually mining salt.

Today, our consumption of salt is extremely high. We average 2½ teaspoons per person per day, which is more than 20 times what we need.

Salt plays an important role in the curing of most meats and sausages, especially dry-cured sausages. Salt not only helps preserve but also adds flavor and acts as a binding agent. In addition, it helps destroy trichinosis in dry and semidry pork sausages and meats.

Always use a good grade of canning or pickling salt, or kosher salt. Do *not* use iodized salt; it can change the flavor and the way salt works. Be sure to use the salt called for in the recipe: the weight of 1 tablespoon of granulated salt is different from 1 tablespoon of kosher salt. Keep salt in closed containers; if not kept sealed, it may absorb moisture and become lumpy.

Sweeteners. Most people have a love affair with sweets, and a touch of sweetness, combined with the salty flavor of many smoked foods, is hard to resist.

Like salt, sweeteners have a long history. The earliest substances used to sweeten food were honey and fruit. Maple syrup was extracted by Native Americans before the arrival of the Europeans. The Greeks learned of sugar during Alexander the Great's invasion; the Persians knew of it by 510 B.C.

Early sugar was a crude, sticky brown substance, but shortly after the Arabs were introduced to sugar, they established the first refineries. On Columbus's second voyage in 1493, he took sugarcane to America from the Canary Islands. By the early 18th century, the West Indies became the main source of supply. In the 1800s sugar was more common but was still used only by the rich. About this time, beet sugar came onto the scene and drastically changed the sugar market.

Besides adding a sweet flavor, sugar aids in the curing process, by counteracting the hardening effect of salt. It also encourages the growth of bacteria, which create a little acidity.

Different sweeteners impart slightly different flavors to brines and marinades. Powdered sweeteners include white, brown, and maple sugar. Liquid sweeteners include molasses, sorghum, corn syrup, maple syrup, and honey. If you are substituting sweeteners, keep in mind that honey is sweeter than sugar.

Seasoned salts, spices, and herbs. This is a good category for experimenting. Although certain spices and herbs are commonly associated with certain foods, you do not have to follow tradition. Begin with those you are familiar with and try them in cures and sausage mixtures. Among the more common flavored salts are celery, garlic, onion, and smoke-flavored. Other combinations can be made or purchased.

Numerous spices and herbs can be used in brines, marinades, and sausages. Some have rather subtle flavors; others are strong. Again, you need to experiment with individual flavors and combinations that you enjoy. The following are the more common spices and herbs:

Allspice	Mint
Anise seed	Mustard seed
Basil	Nutmeg and mace
Bay leaf	Oregano
Caraway seed	Paprika, red pepper, and cayenne
Cardamom	pepper
Celery seed	Parsley
Chervil	Pepper
Cinnamon	Poppy seed
Clove	Rosemary
Coriander seed	Saffron
Cumin seed	Sage
Dill and dill seed	Savory
Fennel and fennel seed	Sesame seed
Fenugreek	Star anise
Garlic, onion, chives	Tarragon
Ginger	Thyme
Horseradish	Turmeric
Marjoram	Vanilla

Monosodium glutamate (MSG) is a flavor enhancer that is often added to cures or used in seasoning foods, such as sausage mixes. Since some people have adverse reactions to MSG, we have not added it to any recipe. You can add it yourself, if you like.

Liquids. Although the main ingredient in brine is usually water, you can add fruit juices, wines, hard liquors, and soy sauce.

Marinades can be made from a wide variety of liquids. Although dry wines are frequently used, some recipes call for a sweet wine. Rum, bourbon, and brandy are favorites for some people.

When selecting wines for use in brines and marinades, choose basic ones that you can use in a variety of dishes. Consider keeping burgundy, chablis, dry vermouth, and dry sherry on hand for cooking; there are reasonably priced brands of these popular wines.

We suggest avoiding wines labeled "cooking wines." They have salt added to them, which alters the flavor of the finished dish.

If you will be using a lot of wine, buy it in the larger jugs, then pour the remaining wine into smaller bottles and cork them tightly so that the wine retains its flavor.

In cooking with wine you don't need to worry about the alcohol, since heat causes it to evaporate; only the flavor will remain. (The same process occurs with vanilla, lemon, and almond flavorings, all of which are very high in alcohol content.) You can substitute fruit juices. For instance, apple cider makes a good substitute for apple wine.

CURES

A *cure* commonly means the ingredients, either in dry form or in a brine, used to treat meat and fish prior to smoking. The cure might be just salt, or salt and water, or it may contain a variety of other seasonings. To be a true cure, the dry cure or brine needs to contain sodium nitrite and sodium nitrate. Sometimes *cure* can also mean potassium nitrite or potassium nitrate, which is the saltpeter commonly used in sausage making. Basically, a nitrate must break down and produce a nitrite, which in turn produces the nitric oxide that actually cures the meat.

In this book, we use the word *cure* in a general sense to mean a mixture that may or may not include nitrite. When we use the term *salt,* we mean sodium chloride, unless otherwise specified.

At one time, hard-curing was the only method used to preserve meat. The meat was placed in a container with just salt. Over a period of a few days, the salt would draw moisture out of the meat, producing a brine. The liquid was drained off, more salt was added, and the process was repeated several times until the meat was hard and dry. The final product would keep indefinitely but had to be soaked in fresh water several times to rid it of salt before it was edible.

Today's curing process takes much less time. In addition, our cured meats are less salty, softer, and often a bit sweeter. Instead of salting and drying meat to a leather-like consistency, we use a cure, usually containing both salt and sugar, to preserve it. Very often, spices and herbs are added, too. To make a brine, water and occasionally other liquids are added to the dry ingredients. If the meat is cold-smoked, the cure—either wet or dry—should also contain curing salts.

The easiest way to add curing salts to a brine, dry cure, or sausage mixture is to use one of the commercially packaged cures that contain the correct ratio of nitrite to salt. There are also packaged cure mixes called "complete cures" that contain salt, nitrite, sugar, spices, and herbs. These are marketed for curing specific foods, such as smoked fish, jerky, and various sausages. For any of these mixtures, be sure to follow the manufacturer's directions exactly; different mixtures are specially formulated for different amounts of meat. Cure mixes can be obtained from some butcher supply houses, sausage makers, meat-processing plants, and feed stores. Small packages of complete cures are available at some supermarkets and butcher shops. Some places, such as butcher supply houses, carry a full line of all kinds of cures, curing agents, spices, and everything needed for curing and smoking meats and making sausages. Check the Yellow Pages in your local phone book.

To preserve meat by curing and smoking, you must first remove some of the water in the meat. Otherwise, spoilage will occur. Salt extracts most of this moisture, and also helps prevent bacterial growth. Because salt alone hardens meat and makes it very salty, you can add sugar or some other sweetener to the cure to soften the hardening effect of the salt, as well as to add flavor. For additional flavor, you can also add spices and herbs.

Curing salts stabilize the meat's color, giving it a pleasing pink or reddish color. The curing salts and carbon compounds combine with the meat pigments to create the characteristic color of smoked meats.

Saltpeter (potassium nitrate) once was used in many sausage recipes and cures as a preservative. In 1975, the U.S. Department of Agriculture banned saltpeter in smoked and cooked meats and sausages, though it is still allowed in very small amounts in dry-cured meats, such as some salamis. We do not recommend the use of saltpeter in food, since it may be harmful to your health.

Curing salts are critical to preventing food poisoning in meats, particularly those that are cold-smoked, such as dry and semidry sausages. Nitrites are used to give meat color, prolong preservation, help protect meat from rancidity and botulism, and give the distinctive flavors we associate with such processed meats as ham and bacon. Without nitrite, hams would just be salty roast pork, and bacon would be simply salt pork. Nitrite, found in all curing salts, does the best job of preserving if we don't want to go through the long process of making hard-cure, dry, salty meats.

During the 1970s, there were alarming news stories about nitrites and the possibility that they produce cancer-causing compounds. An investigation by the National Science Foundation found that nitrites did not cause problems in cured meats, with the possible exception of those commonly cooked quickly at high temperatures, such as bacon. The amount of both nitrate and nitrite that can be used in commercially cured foods is federally regulated, and studies are still being conducted.

According to some experts, any food that is smoked at temperatures below about 140 degrees F should be cured first.

To learn more about nitrites and nitrates, write for the following: "Animal and Plant Health Inspection Service (9 CFR parts 318-381) Nitrates, Nitrites and Salt," U.S.D.A. Animal and Plant Inspections Service, Washington, D.C. 20250.

After using nitrite, be sure to wash any utensils that have come in contact with the cure. Fresh sausages will acquire an unappetizing gray color if they touch the cure. If possible, make the fresh sausage first, then make those that need cures.

Some sausage recipes suggest ascorbic acid as a preserving agent; this is not recommended since it is *not* a curing agent. Although ascorbic acid helps give meat a pleasing color, it does little, if anything, to prevent botulism.

Similarly, some recipes call for a combination of ascorbic acid and a wine or liquor, presumably to help destroy or prevent unwanted bacteria. Liquors and wines should be used only to add flavor and moisture.

Dry cures. A dry cure is sprinkled on or rubbed into the meat to extract moisture. After the prescribed curing time, the meat is rinsed, air-dried, then smoked. Or, if the meat is being cured by salt only, the accumulated liquid is drained off, more salt is added, and the process is repeated.

Here's one dry-cure method: Mix the cure, then rub it thoroughly into each piece of meat, especially around the bones and joints. Spread a layer of cure on the bottom of the container, then alternate the meat and the cure, keeping the largest pieces of meat on the bottom. Cover the meat thoroughly with the mixture. Leave about four days in a cool place, then remove the meat, reapply the cure, and repack. When the curing time is over, rinse the meat well in cold water, then air-dry and smoke it. One pound of dry cure mix should be sufficient for about 12 pounds of meat.

If you are making jerky or hot-smoked fish, try this method: Rub the dry cure into the meat and let it stand overnight. Then rinse, dry, and smoke.

Brines. For a brine, liquid is added to the dry cure. Brines are also called sweet pickling cures, or wet cures. Some people feel brines mix more uniformly, penetrate the meat better, and give the food a less salty taste than do dry cures. Basic brines consist of water, salt, and sugar. If necessary, curing salts are also included.

As a precaution, first boil the water for your brine, then let it cool, or use bottled water. Chlorinated water can have a strange flavor, and the bacteria in some water can cause an off flavor in the brine and food. Sometimes certain bacteria can cause the brine to become slimy.

While brining, especially for more than a few hours, keep the mixture between 38 and 40 degrees F. Cooler temperatures can halt the curing action; on the other hand, warmer temperatures can activate harmful bacteria.

If the brine has an off odor or shows signs of mold or scum, discard it and prepare a fresh batch. If you are thinking about reusing a brine, keep in mind that the ingredients are so economical compared to the cost of meat that it makes more sense to make a fresh batch each time. If you still choose to reuse a brine, check it with a salinometer to determine its strength and add more salt and other dry ingredients if necessary. Do not reuse brine that has been used for fish or strong, gamy meats, since the flavors will transfer to the next batch of meat. (For the same reason, it is also not a good idea to brine several kinds of meat together.) If you want to reuse a brine, freeze it immediately after using to prevent spoilage.

Before smoking brined meats, you should air-dry them until the surface of the meat acquires a glaze (called a pellicle). If you like, you can set up a fan in front of the meat to speed up the drying process. Air-drying helps preserve the meat and gives a pleasing appearance to the finished product.

Injection or pumping. Larger pieces of meat are often pumped or injected with the brine before they are put into the container of brine or before a dry cure is applied. This procedure ensures that the brine reaches the inside of the meat, especially the area around the bone, which is especially susceptible to spoilage if it isn't properly cured. In addition, it allows the interior of the meat to start to cure at the same time as the outer portion.

A special type of large pump (syringe) for this process is available at butcher supply houses. Sterilize the pump and needle before each use. To prevent air from being injected into the meat, fill the pump and needle completely with the brine solution. You will need about 1½ ounces of brine for each pound of meat. Be sure to inject the brine around the bones.

MARINADES

Marinades are used primarily to add flavor. Although many people prefer the taste of meat by itself, others enjoy the change of flavors that marinades produce. A basic recipe for a roast can easily be varied just by using different marinades before the meat is smoked or cooked.

In addition to adding flavor, marinades help prevent meats from drying out. Marinades that contain oil add a coating that also helps keep the meat moist while it is cooking. For more flavor and moisture, inject the meat with a portion of the marinade.

Marinades can be very simple mixtures containing only a few ingredients, or they may call for a long list of herbs, spices, and vegetables. Some contain cooked vegetables, though most are a combination of uncooked foods.

The wine, vinegar, citrus juice, or tomato juice called for in some recipes tenderizes the meat. The longer you marinate the meat, the more tender it will become. A tough cut of meat may need about 48 hours in an acidic marinade.

A spicy marinade can be a real asset if you have big game meat that is too strong. Before smoking or cooking, soak the meat in vinegar water, then marinate it for a couple of days. Or put the meat in a strong, spicy brine, then make it into jerky. You can also grind the meat and make it into spicy sausages. Any of these methods should mask the strong gamy flavor. Keep in mind, however, that a marinade used for very strong meat should not be reused, since the strong flavors will imbue the new piece of meat.

When marinating, allow about 1 cup of marinade for each pound of meat. Marinate the meat in a tightly closed plastic bag, glass, crockery, or enameled container. Do not use metal other than stainless steel; the reaction of some ingredients to the metal can produce a bad taste.

If you are marinating meat for only a couple of hours, you can leave the bowl out at room temperature. If the weather is warm or the meat needs to marinate for a longer period, use the refrigerator.

It is not necessary to rinse marinated meats before cooking or smoking. Take them directly from the marinade to the roasting pan or the cooking rack of the smoker.

If you add the marinade to the water pan when smoke-cooking, you will have a flavorful base for a sauce or gravy at the end of cooking time. (Just be sure you don't let the water pan go dry and burn the juices.) The flavors are concentrated, so a little goes a long way.

Feel free to substitute any of the following marinades for those in the section of recipes for specific meats.

Dry Cure for Fish

The brown sugar of this flavorful cure is especially good with salmon and steelhead, though it is also excellent with other fish. This recipe makes enough cure for approximately 10 pounds of fish. Use it for fillets, steaks, or whole small fish.

1 C pickling salt
1 C packed brown sugar
¾ tsp. pepper
½ tsp. ground allspice
½ tsp. ginger
½ tsp. crumbled bay leaf
2 garlic cloves, pressed

Combine the ingredients, and rub well into fish. Place in a non-metal container for several hours or overnight, depending on the size and amount of fish. Rinse fish well in cold water, rubbing slightly to release excess salt. Pat dry, then allow to air-dry for several hours until fish acquires a glaze. Smoke according to your smoker's directions.

Peppery Dry Cure for Oily Fish

If you enjoy a strong peppery flavor and a dry cure mix, try this one. Pepper is complementary to oily fish.

2⅓ C pickling salt
¾ C light brown sugar
8 tsp. black pepper
6 tsp. ground allspice

Combine the dry cure ingredients, and rub well into the fish. Place in a container, cover lightly, and refrigerate overnight. The next day, rinse, then place on racks to air-dry before smoking.

Spicy Dry Cure for Fish

This recipe makes enough for 20 pounds of large fillets.

- 2 lbs. pickling salt
- 1 lb. brown sugar
- 4 tsp. ground allspice
- 4 tsp. ground cloves
- 4 tsp. ground mace
- 4 tsp. coarse ground pepper
- 2 tbsp. onion powder
- 2 tbsp. garlic powder
- Curing salts (optional)

Combine ingredients. Dredge steaks or fillets in mixture. Place in a container and cover lightly. Refrigerate 8 to 12 hours, then rinse fish well. Pat with paper towels and air-dry on racks or hang until fish acquires a glaze. (This may take up to 6 hours with large fillets.) Hot-smoke until fish is as dry as you like it.

Dry Cure for Jerky

The pickling spices in this mixture add extra flavor. This recipe is also good for fish. Read Jerky before proceeding.

- 2½ C pickling salt
- ½ C sugar
- 1½ tbsp. garlic powder
- 1½ tbsp. onion powder
- 2 tbsp. pickling spices, ground up
- 1½ tsp. celery seed, crushed
- 1 tsp. mustard seed, crushed
- 1 tsp. black pepper

Combine ingredients. Rub mixture well into both sides of the meat strips, then hot-smoke according to the directions for your smoker.

Bay Leaf Brine for Fish

Bay leaves lend a special pungent flavor to the brine. If you live in an area where myrtlewood grows, you can substitute the leaves of the myrtlewood tree for bay leaves. They are very much alike, yet have their own distinctive aroma and flavor. This recipe can be used for fillets, steaks, or whole small fish.

   3 C cold water
1½ C pickling salt
 ¾ C packed brown sugar
   1 tbsp. coarse ground black pepper
   6 bay leaves
1½ tsp. whole allspice
1½ tsp. whole cloves
   2 tsp. ground ginger
   2 garlic cloves, pressed

Combine ingredients. Brine overnight, then rinse in cold water. Pat dry, and allow to air-dry several hours before smoking.

Tarragon Brine for Fish

Tarragon has a strong, distinctive flavor; nevertheless, feel free to substitute other herbs. This recipe is a good choice for anyone on a sugar-free diet. You can use fillets, steaks, or whole small fish.

   2 quarts water
 ½ C pickling salt
   2 tbsp. dry tarragon leaves

Combine ingredients. Brine fish overnight. Rinse in cold water, pat dry, then allow to dry several hours before smoking.

Sweet Pickle Brine for Fish

This is a basic brine with a curing agent added. It may also be used for other meats.

2½ gallons water
2 C pickling salt
2 C brown sugar
4 tsp. Prague Powder #1
4 tsp. coarse ground black pepper
4 tsp. crushed bay leaves

Combine ingredients. Brine the fish, rinse, pat dry, and allow to air-dry before smoking.

Basic Brine for Red Meats

The lemon juice in this brine is good for meats that are somewhat fatty, such as bear, javelina, wild boar, or pork. Use this recipe for thick steaks, roasts, or chops.

2 quarts water
½ C pickling salt
½ C sugar
¼ C lemon juice

Combine ingredients. Brine meat overnight. Rinse in cold water, pat dry, and let air-dry for several hours before smoking.

Cranapple Brine for Birds

Brown sugar, herbs, and cranberry juice seem just right for birds, especially the wild ones. Don't be timid about trying this brine on poultry and pork, however.

> ½ C brown sugar
> ½ C pickling salt
> 4 C cranapple juice
> 1 tsp. dried basil
> 1 tsp. dried thyme

Place cleaned bird in brine overnight. Remove from brine. Pat dry and let air-dry for an hour or more before smoking.

Maple Brine for Birds

Real maple syrup has a special flavor that imitation syrup just can't match, so you'll need to splurge on a bottle of the real thing for this brine. Serve up squares of hot corn bread with maple syrup to go with the smoked birds. This recipe is good for both domestic and wild birds.

> 3 C water
> 1 C dry vermouth
> ⅓ C real maple syrup
> ½ C pickling salt
> 1 bay leaf, crumbled
> 2 tbsp. finely minced onion
> 2 garlic cloves, pressed
> 1 tsp. celery seed, crushed
> 1 tbsp. fresh ground pepper

Combine ingredients. Brine birds overnight. Remove from brine, rinse in cold water, pat dry, and let air-dry for an hour or more, until the birds have acquired a glaze.

Brine for Wild Meats

The many strong flavors of this recipe make it a great brine for fattier meats or for those meats that are a bit stronger than you prefer. Try it on antelope, mountain goat, javelina, bear, or wild boar, but don't overlook beef and wild game birds.

  ¼ C pickling salt
  ¼ C sugar
  2 C cold water
  1 C apple wine
  1 C soy sauce
  2 tbsp. brandy
  2 tsp. grated fresh ginger root
  2 tsp. grated fresh orange peel
10 juniper berries, crushed
  1 tbsp. onion juice
  2 tsp. garlic juice
  1 tsp. hot sauce such as Tabasco

Combine ingredients. Marinate roast or steaks all day or overnight. Rinse lightly, pat dry, and let air-dry before smoking.

Venison Brine

Peppercorns, juniper berries, and red wine are essential.

  2 gallons water
  1 C pickling salt
  1 C sugar
  3 bay leaves
10 peppercorns, crushed
12 juniper berries, crushed
  1 tsp. chili powder
  1 C dry red wine

Combine ingredients. Brine meat overnight. Rinse, pat dry, and let air-dry before smoking.

Brine for Wild Game

This recipe is excellent for venison, elk, moose, bear, antelope, sheep, and reindeer.

- 1 pint cider vinegar
- 1 quart water
- 1 C noniodized salt
- 1 tbsp. black peppercorns
- ½ C brown sugar
- 1 blade mace
- 2 tbsp. butter
- ¼ tbsp. parsley
- 2 medium onions, chopped
- 1 medium carrot, sliced
- 1 C dry red wine

Bring all ingredients, except for wine, to a boil. Reduce heat, then simmer for 30 minutes. Strain into a large nonmetal container and add wine. Use immediately; do not store. Brine meat 3 to 4 days in the refrigerator, turning often to ensure even penetration. (Recipe from Luhr Jensen and Sons.)

Citrus and Spice Marinade

This is Lue's favorite marinade for big game meats and beef. It is very flavorful and makes a wonderful seasoning for kabobs. It is also a good choice if your game meat has a stronger taste than you prefer.

¼ C soy sauce
¼ C orange juice
¼ C lemon juice
1 tsp. salt
1 tsp. ground turmeric
1 tsp. ground coriander
½ tsp. ground ginger
1 garlic clove, minced
1 tbsp. packed brown sugar
2 tbsp. minced onion
2 tbsp. oil

Combine all ingredients, stirring until sugar is dissolved. Marinate meat several hours or overnight. Reserve marinade, heat, and serve alongside cooked meat.

Salt-Free Marinade

This is a good marinade for those on salt-free diets since it has plenty of flavor without salt. Feel free to use different herbs.

1 C burgundy
½ C olive oil
¼ C chopped parsley
1 tsp. dry marjoram leaves
1 bay leaf

Marinate the meat for several hours or overnight. Do not rinse before cooking.

Burgundy Marinade

This is a traditional red wine marinade for red meats.

- ½ C olive oil
- ¼ C minced fresh parsley
- ⅛ tsp. dry tarragon leaves
- ⅛ tsp. dry thyme leaves
- 1 bay leaf
- 1 C burgundy

Combine all ingredients. Marinate the meat for at least 24 hours.

Marinade for Liver

You can use a liver marinade to enhance the distinctive flavor of liver, or to mask it.

- ½ C olive oil
- ⅛ tsp. garlic salt
- ⅛ tsp. pepper
- ¼ tsp. crushed marjoram leaves

Combine ingredients and marinate liver.

Cooked Barbecue Marinade

Every recipe file should contain at least one good recipe for barbecue sauce, and this might become your favorite. It is a good choice for large and small game animals, beef, heart, or liver. This marinade is especially good for any meat that is on the fatty side, such as bear, javelina, or pork.

    2 C cold water
    2 C dry red wine
    2 tbsp. lemon juice
    1 4-oz. can tomato paste
    ¼ C sugar
    1 onion, diced
    2 carrots, diced
    4 celery ribs, diced
    2 garlic cloves, pressed
    1 tsp. hot sauce, such as Tabasco
    2 tsp. prepared horseradish
    1 tsp. mustard
    1 bay leaf
    1 tsp. crushed thyme
    2 tbsp. minced fresh parsley

Combine all ingredients. Simmer over low heat, stirring occasionally, until vegetables are soft and flavors combined, about 1 hour. Cool, then refrigerate for a full day before using. Marinate a roast in the sauce for 24 hours. Heat remaining sauce to serve with the cooked meat.

Herbed Cooked Marinade

A variety of flavors combine to make this marinade a good choice for beef, venison, and small game. Try it with heart and tongue, too.

¼ C olive oil
1 carrot, diced
1 rib celery, diced
1 onion, diced
3 garlic cloves, pressed
1 C water
3 C dry red wine
1 tsp. Worcestershire sauce
½ tsp. crushed thyme
½ tsp. crushed marjoram
1 bay leaf
1 tsp. whole cloves
1 tbsp. peppercorns
1 tbsp. juniper berries, crushed

In hot olive oil, sauté carrot, celery, onion, and garlic until slightly tender. Add remaining ingredients and simmer, covered, over low heat for 1 hour. Strain, or put in blender or food processor after removing bay leaf. Cool.

Juniper Marinade for Game

This marinade provides some stronger flavors for meats that can handle them. It is suitable for big game, small game, beef, and game birds.

    ¾ C burgundy
    1 C olive oil
    1 tsp. dry tarragon leaves
    1 rib celery, chopped
    1 onion, thinly sliced
    6 peppercorns, crushed
   10 juniper berries, crushed
    ¼ tsp. dry sage leaves
    1 tsp. grated lemon peel

Combine all ingredients. Marinate the meat for at least 24 hours.

Sesame-Soy Marinade

If you enjoy a teriyaki-style marinade, this recipe will soon become your favorite. Lue uses it for stir-fry dishes after marinating thin slices of meat or fish. For a smoke flavor, add a few drops of liquid smoke to the marinade. You can use this recipe for fish, pork, venison, or birds.

    1 tbsp. crushed toasted sesame seeds
    6 tbsp. soy sauce
    2 tbsp. sugar
    2 tbsp. oil
    1 green onion, thinly sliced
    2 garlic cloves, pressed
    2 tsp. grated fresh ginger root
    ⅛ tsp. pepper

Combine ingredients, and marinate meat at least 1½ hours. If smoke-cooking meat, after marinating add the marinade to the water pan, with enough water to fill ⅔ of the pan.

Marinade for Barbecued Pork

Fresh ginger root does not taste at all like the dry powdered version used in baking. If you like to use a lot of fresh ginger, wrap the root very well and place it in the freezer. When you need some, grate the frozen root, using the fine section of your grater. This recipe will handle up to 3 pounds of lean boneless pork, cut into 1-inch-thick slices.

- ¼ C soy sauce
- 2 tbsp. dry sherry
- 2 tbsp. honey
- 2 tbsp. brown sugar
- 1 tsp. salt
- ¼ tsp. each, crushed anise seed, ground cinnamon, and cloves
- 1 tbsp. grated fresh ginger root

Combine marinade ingredients in a saucepan, and heat until sugar is dissolved. Cool before marinating meat.

Ducky Marinade

Try this marinade for domestic or wild ducks or for geese. The red wine will counteract the fat of domestic ducks and complement the stronger flavor of wild ducks. This recipe is for two ducks.

- ½ C soy sauce
- 2 tbsp. brown sugar
- 1 onion, chopped
- ½ C Pinot Noir burgundy, or other dry red wine
- 1 tbsp. grated fresh ginger root
- 2 garlic cloves, pressed
- 2 bay leaves, broken up

Mix marinade. Place ducks, either whole or split in half, in a plastic bag, and pour marinade over them. Let marinate overnight, turning several times to ensure that all parts are marinated.

Marinade for Fish

We like this marinade for white-fleshed fish. The mild flavors enhance the fish. This marinade is good for either lean or oily fish.

    1 C dry vermouth
    4 peppercorns, crushed
    2 tsp. grated lemon peel
    ¼ C chopped parsley
    ¼ C oil

Combine all ingredients, then marinate the fish for at least half an hour.

Spicy Marinade for Shellfish

Although it is difficult to improve the succulent flavors of shellfish, this marinade is a pleasant change. It also works well as a dipping sauce.

    ½ C olive oil
    ¼ C lime juice
    1 C rice wine vinegar
    2 tbsp. chopped fresh cilantro
    2 garlic cloves, pressed
    1 tsp. oil
    1 tsp. red chili paste
       Salt to taste

Combine all ingredients and add the shellfish. (For example, two dozen large shrimp that have been shelled and deveined.) Marinate 30 minutes before smoke-cooking.

Domestic Meats
and
Fowl

Y ou can prepare any domestic meat by those methods that fully cook the meat, such as barbecuing, smoke-cooking, or hot-smoking.

Barbecue grills usually cook foods at relatively high temperatures without imparting much smoky flavor. Smoke-cooking both smokes and cooks the food, as the name implies.

Hot-smoking cooks most smaller cuts, but because temperatures are usually lower than with barbecues, roasts, chickens, and turkeys may need to finish cooking in the range oven after they are smoked. The extent to which foods are cooked during the hot-smoking process depends, in large part, on the unit being used and how hot it gets.

Hot-smoking is also used to add smoke flavor to foods that are already cooked. For example, you might cook pork chops to the well-done stage, then hot-smoke them for half an hour to give them a light smoke flavor.

Meats should be cured before cold-smoking, since the temperature is not high enough to cook the meat.

Cooking pork. Because of the danger of trichinosis (see Safety and Health), pork should always be cooked well-done. Freezing pork to U.S.D.A. standards will also kill the trichinosis parasite: freeze at

-20 degrees F for 6 to 12 days, -10 degrees F for 10 to 20 days, or -5 degrees F for 20 to 30 days. Fresh pork should not be used for making jerky: it is too fatty to make a good jerky, and more important, jerky is dried but not really cooked. Dry and semidry sausages that are cold-smoked or matured are an exception to the rule about cooking pork. The salt, curing agent, temperature, and humidity all play a part in ensuring the safety and edibility of these products.

Cooking poultry. Poultry needs special consideration because it is more perishable than beef. Use fresh birds as quickly as possible, or freeze them. Always thaw frozen birds completely in the refrigerator before cooking.

Choose plump, firm birds. Domestic birds sold in the market are usually cleaned and plucked; all you have to do is rinse the poultry and prepare it for cooking or smoking.

Large turkeys are often a good buy. If you do not intend to use the entire turkey at once, the butcher can cut it. Or smoke the turkey first, then cut it up, package it into individual meals, and store it in the freezer. The bones and scraps can be used to make a delicious stock.

We have a preference for smoke-cooked turkey breasts. These cuts are available whole or cut in half, and they provide a lot of meat with little bone.

Domestic ducks and geese are fat birds that can be treated about the same as other poultry. A marinade or brine containing wine, tomato juice, or citrus juice is a good choice for these birds, since the acid counteracts the fat.

One delicious way to add smoke flavor to any bird is to hot-smoke it for about an hour, then cook it using your favorite recipe. This method reduces cooking time by about 20 percent and gives a light smoky flavor to the meat.

Birds do not have to be cured before they are hot-smoked, smoke-cooked, or smoke-flavored. If they are going to be cold-smoked, however, they should be cured in a brine containing curing salts. In fact, you should also cure a large bird if it is going to be hot-smoked at the low end of the temperature range (below about 165 degrees F).

A cured bird can be cooked or smoked by most methods. You may want to cure a bird before roasting it in the oven just because you enjoy the flavor that a brine with curing salts gives to the meat. Cured and smoked poultry has a flavor similar to that of ham.

Brining a bird without a cure takes about the same length of time as brining it with a cure. It should be rinsed well, then air-dried before being smoked. Marinating a large bird can take anywhere from overnight to several days. A marinated bird can go directly into the cooker, oven, or hot-smoker.

Curing poultry. To cure a bird, rinse it well, then submerge it up to five days in a cold brine that contains curing salts. Keep refrigerated or otherwise chilled during the entire brining time. The length of time it takes to cure depends on the size of the bird: a large turkey will take a maximum of five days; a chicken will take one or two days (see the table Approximate Brining Times at the back of this book). The brine should be stirred several times during the curing process.

Pumping or injecting some of the brine into large birds will halve the curing time. Pump into the bird a brine mixture equal in weight to about 10 percent of the bird's weight. After pumping, submerge in the cold brine.

When the brining time is up, rinse the bird, pat it dry, and put it on a rack or hang it for an hour or more to air-dry. Air-drying will allow it to acquire a glaze before it is smoked. To present an attractive bird on the table, especially a large one, put it in a stockinette before cooking or smoking. A stockinette is a mesh tube or sack slipped over a bird to keep the wings and legs close to the body during cooking and smoking. Stockinettes are available from butcher supply shops.

There are many ways to cook or smoke a bird. Although the following instructions are for a 20-pound turkey, the same methods can be used with smaller turkeys, chickens, and parts of turkeys.

Oven-roasting cured turkey. To get a smoked flavor, you can either add liquid smoke to the cure, or smoke the turkey in a smoker before cooking. To cook the bird, first place it in a large pan in the oven preheated to 165 degrees F. Leave the door cracked to allow moisture to escape. When the turkey appears dry on the surface— about two hours—close the oven door, turn up the temperature to 250 degrees F, and roast the turkey until it tests done. A meat thermometer stuck into the thickest part of the breast (not touching bone) will read 180 to 185 degrees F when the turkey is done. You can also tell the meat is done if the leg joint moves easily.

Oven-roasting marinated or uncured turkey. This is a basic recipe for roasting a turkey. If you like, you can add a smoked flavor, either by adding liquid smoke to the marinade, or smoking the turkey in a smoker before roasting.

As a general rule, roast turkeys in an oven preheated to 325 degrees F; allow 18 minutes per pound.

Rinse and dry the thawed bird. If you plan to stuff the turkey, do so just before it goes into the oven. Place several layers of cheesecloth over the turkey to keep the skin from drying out and baste the bird generously with melted butter, margarine, or oil. Baste frequently as it roasts.

Hot-smoking turkey. Since we can't give directions for all types of smoker units, we've chosen the small electric smokehouse as an example. Follow the manufacturer's directions for your unit.

Brine or marinate the bird, if desired. Let it air-dry for an hour or more. Open the bird's cavity to allow the smoke inside. Preheat the smoker, then smoke the bird for two to four hours, depending on how heavy a smoke flavor you want. Use one panful of chips each hour. Then transfer the smoked turkey from the smoker to a preheated 325-degree oven and roast it; decrease the cooking time by about 10 percent for each hour the turkey was in the smoker. If you will be stuffing the turkey, have the dressing ready and heated, then stuff the bird just before putting it into the oven. Increase the roasting time to compensate for the dressing.

Smoke-cooking turkey. Brine or marinate the turkey. Let it air-dry for at least an hour. Or just sprinkle the turkey with salt and pepper or other seasonings.

Prop open the cavity to allow the smoke to penetrate. Place soaked wood chunks on the heat source. If you use a water pan, put it on the rack in the smoker, then fill it with hot water, or water flavored with wine, stock, fruit juice, herbs, and spices. Or use the marinade, if the turkey was marinated. Check the water pan about every three to four hours, and add more liquid, if needed.

Place the turkey on an oiled cooking rack above the water pan. Allow about one hour per pound to smoke-cook the bird. (Cooking time may vary, so follow the manufacturer's directions for your smoke-cooker.) A meat thermometer inserted in the thickest part of the breast will read 180 to 185 degrees F when the bird is well done.

Cooking and smoking turkey on a gas grill. To prepare the turkey for cooking on a gas grill, brine or marinate the bird. You can also stuff it.

A typical gas grill is fueled by propane or natural gas. To produce smoke, you must add wood. To make a "log," place about 2 cups of soaked wood chips on a rectangle of heavy-duty aluminum foil. Wrap securely, leaving the ends of the log open. Remove the cooking grid, then move the rocks onto half of the grate and place one foil log on the rocks. Preheat the grill for 10 minutes. Place a shallow drip pan filled with water on the empty half of the lava rock grate. Replace the cooking grid over the drip pan and close the hood. When the wet wood chips begin producing smoke, place the turkey on the cooking grid over the drip pan. Roast the turkey over medium heat with the hood closed until a meat thermometer shows an internal temperature of 185 degrees F. (Cooking time will vary depending on the particular unit.) Turn the turkey once, and replace the foil logs as needed for continuous smoking.

Cooking and smoking turkey in a dual chamber smoker. Stuff the turkey, if desired, or brine or marinate. Cook slowly (250 to 275 degrees F on the temperature gauge on the unit) for 45 to 60 minutes per pound. The skin will turn deep brown before the turkey is completely done.

Herbed Beef Roast

Try this for a full-bodied roast with excellent flavor. This recipe applies equally well to venison.

> 4- to 5-lb. beef roast, boneless, tied
> ⅔ C dry red wine
> ½ green bell pepper, finely chopped
> ½ onion, finely chopped
> ⅓ C vegetable oil
> 1 tsp. dry basil leaf, crushed
> 1 tsp. dry oregano leaf, crushed
> 2 tsp. salt
> 2 garlic cloves, pressed

Place the marinade and meat either in a deep nonmetallic bowl or in a plastic sack. (The oven-roasting bags work well.) Turn the meat several times to ensure even marination. Marinate overnight. Remove the meat from the refrigerator 5 to 6 hours before cooking. Insert a meat thermometer into the center of the meat. Or, if your smoke-cooker has an opening on the side, insert the thermometer in the meat after placing it on the grill. Smoke-cook 4 to 5 hours or until thermometer registers your preference of doneness. Cut roast into thin slices. Serves 8 to 10.

Smoked Beef Brisket

A beef brisket is one of the fattier cuts of beef, so you'll end up with more shrinkage than from a lean cut.

> 10-lb. beef brisket

Sprinkle meat with Seasoned Salt (see page 174). Place in the smoker, fat side up, and cook at 350 degrees F for approximately 1 hour per pound.

Smoke-Cooked Barbecue Ribs

Just about everyone likes barbecued ribs, and there is no better way to prepare them than to smoke them while they are cooking.

     4 lbs. spare ribs or pork or beef back ribs

Sauce:
     1 onion, chopped
     1 C catsup
     1 tsp. salt
     ¼ tsp. hot pepper sauce
     1 tbsp. chili powder
     2 C water
     1 tsp. mustard
     2 tbsp. brown sugar

Place ribs in a nonmetal pan, cover with sauce, and refrigerate 6 hours or overnight. Turn occasionally. Smoke-cook according to directions for your unit. It can take anywhere from 2 to 5 hours, depending on the unit and other variables. Remember that pork ribs should be well-done, so they will take longer than beef ribs.

Smoky Meat Loaf

Smoking the meat loaf mixture takes plain meat loaf to new heights.

     3 lbs. lean ground beef
     3 eggs, lightly beaten
    ¼ C rolled oats
    ¼ C toasted wheat germ
     1 8-oz. can tomato sauce
     3 tbsp. packed brown sugar
    2½ tbsp. prepared mustard
    ⅓ C finely chopped onion
    ¼ C finely chopped green bell pepper
     1 tsp. salt
    ¼ tsp. pepper

Combine all ingredients in a large bowl and mix well. Place the meat loaf mixture in the center of a sheet of heavy-duty aluminum foil, 20 to 24 inches long, and shape into a loaf. Fold the edges of the foil down until they are even with the top of the loaf. Place the loaf on the grill of the readied smoke-cooker, and cook about 5 hours. Serves 6 to 8.

Allspice Pork

These unusual flavors will have guests asking for recipes.

    5 lbs. pork loin
    ⅓ C whole allspice
    6 green onions, chopped, including tops
    3 hot peppers, chopped (use with or without seeds,
       depending on how much heat you prefer)
    5 bay leaves
    1 tsp. salt
    ¼ tsp. pepper

Heat whole allspice in a small fry pan, stirring for 5 minutes; then grind or place in a mortar and pound until powdery. Add other seasoning ingredients and grind together to make a thick paste. Using a sharp knife, make a number of deep cuts into the meat. Rub the paste into the pork and push into the cuts. Refrigerate overnight. If smoke-cooking, put the water pan in place; add the remaining marinade and fill with water. Place the meat on an oiled cooking rack and cook until internal temperature reaches 185 degrees F, or well-done on the thermometer.

Sesame Ginger Pork

Although this recipe is for pork, it can also be used for wild boar, javelina, or poultry. Use the remaining marinade as a dipping sauce.

2 lbs. lean pork loin
⅓ C dry sherry
½ C soy sauce
½ C packed brown sugar
2 tbsp. finely grated fresh ginger root
2 tbsp. sesame seeds, lightly toasted
2 tbsp. sesame oil or other cooking oil

Combine marinade ingredients and stir to mix well. Add meat to mixture and marinate 8 to 12 hours. If smoke-cooking, put the water pan in place and fill with water. Cook for about 3 hours or until internal temperature of the meat registers 185 degrees F. Cut into thin slices. Serves 4 to 6.

Note: With both Sesame Ginger Pork and Orange-Soy Pork, the meat can be smoked in an electric smoker. Let it air-dry for an hour after marinating, then smoke in the preheated smokehouse for 2 hours using 2 panfuls of wood chips. Transfer the roast to a kitchen oven preheated to 300 degrees F, and cook for 1½ hours, or until meat thermometer registers 185 degrees F.

Orange-Soy Pork

This recipe and Sesame Ginger Pork are outstanding as main courses or sliced and served as appetizers. For a more pronounced flavor, split the loin in half lengthwise, then cut into 1-inch slices and marinate before smoking. That way, it will take less time to smoke-cook. If you have leftover smoked pork, try cutting it into small chunks or strips and adding it to fried rice, or to vegetables and pasta salads. This marinade is also good for red meats, poultry, and game birds.

    2 lbs. lean pork loin
    1 C orange juice
    1 C dry sherry
    1 C soy sauce
    1 tbsp. catsup
    2 tbsp. sugar
    2 garlic cloves, pressed

Combine marinade ingredients and stir to mix well. Add meat to mixture and marinate 8 to 12 hours. If smoke-cooking, put the water pan in place and fill with water. Cook about 3 hours or until internal temperature of the meat reaches 185 degrees F.

Leg of Lamb

This makes an impressive meal for lamb lovers.

    1 5-lb. leg of lamb
    2 garlic cloves
    1 onion
    ½ tsp. dry crushed marjoram
    ½ tsp. dry crushed rosemary
    ¾ C dry red wine
       Salt and pepper

With a small, sharp knife, cut several slits in top of lamb. Grind the garlic, onion, and herbs together, and push mixture into the slits. Sprinkle the entire lamb with salt and pepper. Smoke-cook about 5 hours, basting with wine several times. If using a water pan, fill mostly with water, then add some wine and a teaspoon or so of the herbs.

Lamb Kabobs

This recipe is based on memories of a delectable lamb kabob and rice pilaf dinner served at a delightful little Armenian restaurant.

>   2 lbs. boneless lamb
>   2 to 3 onions
>   2 green bell peppers
> ⅓ C vegetable oil
>   2 garlic cloves, pressed
> ¼ C minced parsley
> ¼ C lemon juice
>   1 tsp. crushed rosemary leaves
>   1 tsp. salt
> ¼ tsp. pepper

Cut meat into 1½-inch cubes. Quarter the onions. Seed and cut each pepper into 8 chunks. Combine marinade ingredients; add meat cubes and vegetables, and stir well to coat completely. Cover and refrigerate for several hours or overnight. Thread meat onto skewers. If using a water pan, add the marinade to the pan. Place the kabobs on the oiled grill or place them on a sheet of aluminum foil that has been perforated. Cover and smoke-cook about 2½ hours. Thread the onion and peppers (and other vegetables if you wish*) onto separate skewers, brush them with marinade, and place them in the smoker the last hour of cooking. Serves 4 to 6.

*Other vegetables that go well with lamb include red bell peppers, cherry tomatoes, and mushrooms.

Apple Wine Smoked Ham

A tasty way to jazz up a cooked ham is to give it some extra smoke flavor, plus a taste of cloves, apple wine, or cider, and top if off with a pineapple-apricot glaze.

> 1 fully cooked ham
>   Whole cloves
> 1 quart apple wine or cider

Score the fat side of ham to make diamond shapes, then place a whole clove in the center of each diamond. Put the water pan in place. Add the wine by pouring it over the ham into the pan below. Smoke-cook 3 to 4 hours, depending on the unit and size of ham. During the last hour of cooking, brush the ham with the following glaze. (Remember, each time the lid is removed to apply glaze you lose about 15 minutes of cooking time.)

Glaze:

> ½ C pineapple-apricot jam
> 1 tbsp. prepared mustard
> 1 tsp. lemon juice

Ginger Chicken

There are certain flavors that go especially well with certain foods. Citrus, soy, and ginger are especially good with poultry and pork.

      1 large chicken
      ¾ C commercial barbecue sauce
      ¼ C orange juice
      2 tbsp. brown sugar, packed
      1 tbsp. grated fresh ginger root

Combine the marinade ingredients in a nonmetal bowl. Add the chicken and spread the marinade all over the chicken, inside and out. Let marinate several hours or overnight. If smoke-cooking, use a water pan and add some herbs. Place the chicken on the oiled cooking rack. Cover and cook approximately 3 hours. Serves 4.

Citrus Chicken

This is Lue's favorite marinade for birds. It is tangy, sweet, salty, and garlicky—an excellent complement for poultry and many other meats.

      1 6-lb. roasting chicken
      ¼ C oil
      1 C orange juice (prepared, not concentrated)
         Juice of 1 large lemon
      ¼ C honey
      ¼ C parsley
      ¼ C soy sauce
      1 tbsp. dry mustard
      2 to 3 garlic cloves, pressed

Combine marinade ingredients in a saucepan and heat. Pour over chicken in a nonmetal bowl. Spoon the marinade into the bird cavity. Let stand several hours or overnight, turning several times. If using a water pan, add the marinade to it. Place the chicken on the oiled cooking rack and smoke-cook 6 to 7 hours, or until the leg moves easily at the joint. Serves 4 to 6.

Yogurt Chicken

Yogurt is a great tenderizer and moisturizer. Experiment with plain yogurt, and add your favorite herbs and spices. You may also want to try some of the flavored yogurts.

    4 skinned chicken breast halves
    1 C plain yogurt
    ½ tsp. grated nutmeg
    ½ tsp. ground cinnamon
    2 tsp. grated lemon rind
    ½ tsp. salt
    ¼ C minced green onion

Combine yogurt and seasonings in a large bowl and mix well. Place the chicken in the mixture, and turn meat over to coat on all sides. Cover and let stand while preparing smoker. When ready to cook, place the coated chicken on the oiled grill. Cover and smoke-cook 3 to 4 hours. Serves 2 to 4.

Smoked Piña Colada Chicken Breasts

If you enjoy the flavors of rum, coconut, and pineapple, this recipe is for you.

    4   whole chicken breasts, boned
    1   sweet onion
    1   6-oz. can pineapple juice, concentrated
    ⅔   C coconut milk, or water
    ⅓   C rum
    2   tsp. lemon juice
    2   tbsp. brown sugar
    ¼   tsp. each rubbed sage, crushed basil, thyme, and marjoram,
        or 1 tsp. poultry seasoning
    ½   tsp. salt
    1   tbsp. oil

Combine all ingredients except for chicken and onion. Place chicken in shallow baking dish and smoke for 1 hour. Place onion slices over chicken; pour sauce over the top and smoke another hour.

Smoked Bird with Ham and Cheese

This recipe is good for boned breast meat of turkey, chicken, pheasant, grouse, and other birds. Remember that the meat must be sliced and smoked before you begin. If you are using a small electric smokehouse, smoke with 1 pan full of flavored chips.

- 6 large slices uncooked, smoked bird breast
- 6 thin slices cooked ham
- 6 ounces Swiss cheese, cut into 6 sticks
- ¼ C flour
- 2 tbsp. margarine or butter
- 1 tsp. chicken bouillon granules
- 1 C sliced fresh mushrooms
- ⅓ C sauterne or dry vermouth
- 2 tbsp. flour
- Toasted sliced almonds

Place smoked slices on cutting board. Working from center out, pound lightly with wooden mallet to make cutlets about ¼ inch thick. Place a ham slice and a cheese stick on each cutlet. Tuck in sides and roll each up as you would for a jelly roll, pressing to seal well. Skewer or tie securely. Coat rolls with flour, brown in butter, then place them in a baking pan.

In the same skillet, combine ½ C water, then bouillon, mushrooms, and wine. Heat, stirring well. Pour mixture over rolls in baking pan. Cover and bake at 350 degrees F until tender, or about 1 hour. Transfer rolls to warm platter. Blend 2 tbsp. flour with ½ C cold water; stir into drippings in baking pan. Cook and stir until thickened. Pour a little gravy over the rolled breasts; garnish with almonds. Serve remaining gravy. Serves 3 to 6.

Game Meats
and
Game Birds

The flavors of game meats, ranging as they do from subtle to distinctive, open up a whole new realm of possibilities for the home cook. The methods of smoke cooking and the recipes in this chapter are intended to enhance the taste of game, though some recipes also work well with domestic meats. To make the most of your game, pay careful attention to its care before it reaches your kitchen. Many books give details on the care of game animals in the field. If the process is new to you, we suggest reading up on the subject until you feel comfortable about doing it (see the Bibliography). Or better yet, watch an experienced hunter do it.

BIG GAME
Big game animals include deer, elk, moose, caribou, bison, antelope, bear, mountain sheep, and mountain goat. For the purposes of smoke-cooking, we will treat wild boars and peccaries here, too.

Care. You must begin to care for game meats even before the hunt. Take along the equipment necessary to care for the meat from the time the animal is downed until you're home.

We've frequently heard people say they don't like the gamy flavor of venison; most of this flavor results from improper care.

Once we pulled in to a service station and noticed a car with a nice buck deer tied to the hood. The deer, not even dressed, was already slightly bloated. The car's license plate told us it would probably be another two days before the hunters would be home. We could safely predict that someone would later be complaining that game meat is not fit to eat.

Any game animal should be gutted immediately and the cavity propped open to hasten cooling. Depending on the animal and the situation, including the weather, the animal may be skinned, left whole, quartered, or boned out. Blood-shot meat should be cut away.

There are three key words to remember regarding the care of any game meat: *clean, cool,* and *dry.*

Keep twigs, leaves, and dirt off the meat when the animal is being dressed, cut up, and transported. Even deer hairs, because they are oily, can give an off flavor to the meat.

Use ice or insulation to keep the meat cool. Game meats are highly perishable, and as soon as the animal is dead, bacteria start to multiply. Since warmth speeds this process, it is important to cool the animal quickly. Game animals also spoil rapidly because they are not pumped full of chemicals, as many domestic animals are.

Use tarps or plastic sheets to keep off rain and snow. In the field, do not use water to wash the carcass unless you can dry it thoroughly, since water hastens deterioration.

An ongoing controversy among hunters is whether game meat should be aged. Many say that hanging the carcass meat for two to ten days is beneficial because aging will break down the connective tissue. Others say, however, that since the connective tissue breaks down even while meat is frozen, aging is unnecessary.

Those who recommend no aging, or only a short aging time, point out there is less trimming loss (a long hanging time causes the meat to form a dry, hard crust that needs to be trimmed away before the meat is used), less bacterial growth on the surface of the meat and in gunshot areas, and less shrinkage.

We've tried aging our game animals anywhere from a couple of days to a week; we've also boned it and frozen it immediately. We have found no appreciable difference in eating quality.

In cool weather the cleaned, skinned carcass can be hung in a garage or shed. In warm weather the meat should be hung in a commercial cooler.

If a butcher doesn't cut the meat for you, you will need to learn how to do it properly yourself. Many hunters have learned they get sweeter venison if they bone out the meat rather than cut it with the bone in. When bones are sawed, bone dust and marrow are spread across the cut. Both bone dust and marrow, which goes rancid quickly, contribute to strong flavors.

Many people object to the taste and texture of the fat of some game, especially deer. Deer fat is usually trimmed away and suet or pork fat substituted. Although other big game meat fats aren't so objectionable, in many cases replacing the fat with pork or beef fat results in better flavor.

The next step is to preserve the meat in some manner. Although freezing is by far the most common method these days, there are several options (see Preserving Foods).

Sometimes, despite all the right care, the meat still has strong flavors. If the taste is objectionable, try soaking it in a vinegar-water solution, curing it, smoking it, or using flavorful marinades. If all else fails, you can make sausages or mincemeat out of it.

Cooking big game. Cooking most game meats (for bears, see below) is much the same as cooking their domestic counterparts. The more tender cuts come from the lower back and rump; the less tender cuts are the leg muscles and shoulders.

Since most game meats are lean, some type of fat is usually added during cooking to keep the meat from drying out. Adding fat isn't necessary, however, with moist cooking methods, such as stewing.

Depending on how the game meat is cooked, there are different ways to add fat to the meat to prevent it from drying out.

Larding. Small pieces of pork fat or salt pork, called lardoons, are inserted into slits in the meat. A tool called a larding needle is specially designed for this purpose. The lardoons are put into the needle, and the needle is pushed deep into the meat. When the needle is pulled out, the lardoons stay in the meat. Or you can make slits in the meat with a small, sharp pointed knife, and push small pieces of pork fat into the cuts. Sometimes the fat is marinated before being inserted into the meat to provide additional flavor. Garlic can also be pushed into the slits with the fat. Larding is an especially effective method for large roasts.

Barding. Sheets or strips of salt pork or bacon are laid across the top of the meat to baste it while it cooks. This method works better with small pieces of meat, such as small birds, than with large roasts.

Injection. Injecting meat with a marinade or other seasoned liquids is an excellent way to get moisture and flavor deep inside large pieces of meat. You can buy a syringe specifically designed for this purpose at a specialty kitchen shop or butcher supply house.

Other methods for adding fat or moisture include basting and using sauces. Basting means brushing or spooning liquids (for example, marinades, stock, or meat drippings) or fat over the meat as it is cooking. Before meats are cooked, they can be coated with mayonnaise, salad dressing, yogurt, or a vegetable sauce.

Moist-cooking methods—roasting in a covered pan, braising, stewing, steaming, and poaching—all help retain natural moisture in the food.

You can use more than one method at the same time. For example, you can inject a large roast with a seasoned liquid, marinate it, then bard it before roasting it in a covered pan.

Cooking bear. The palatability of bears varies with the individual animal, the time of year, and the food the bear has been eating. A spring bear that has been living on its food reserves all winter will be leaner than a fall bear that has been fattening up for hibernation. Bears that have been feeding on plants, roots, grubs, and berries taste better than one that has been feasting on spawned-out salmon.

Because bear meat is naturally fatty, most of the extra fat is trimmed away during butchering, and no fat is added when cooking. Bear meat requires no aging, and perhaps because of its fat content, it spoils more quickly than other big game.

Bear fat is frequently saved and rendered for other uses, such as shortening for breads and pie crusts. Some people use bear fat for boot grease.

Since bears, like hogs, may host trichinae and cause trichinosis, you should follow the same rules as for pork. Either cook the meat to the well-done stage, or freeze it according to the recommended U.S.D.A. temperature and times.

Cook bear just as you would fresh pork, that is, until the internal temperature of the meat reaches 185 degrees F. Cooking bear in a microwave is not recommended; since many microwave ovens have cold spots, you can't be sure all parts of the meat will have reached the proper temperature.

Because of the fat content of bear meat, sometimes it helps to oven-cook the meat on a rack so that the fat can drain off. Or you can precook the meat on a rack, drain the fat, then finish with the recipe.

Bear meat is not recommended for jerky, both because the meat is so fat and because jerky is uncooked.

SMALL GAME

Rabbits and squirrels are the most commonly hunted small game animals. Other small game include opossum, raccoon, muskrat, woodchuck, marmot, and beaver.

When cleaning small game animals, watch out for scent glands. They are under the front legs or armpits, or along the spine, or both.

When smoking and cooking these small animals, treat them basically the same as you would chicken or game birds. Some, such as rabbits and squirrels, are lean and need basting; beaver, muskrat, and 'possum, on the other hand, are fatty. Brining helps tenderize the older animals, as do parboiling and other moist-cooking methods.

Rabbit and hare. Rabbits include the various cottontails; hares include jackrabbits, snowshoe and arctic hares, and others. Although taxonomically different, all of them are often called rabbits.

Cottontails are about 2 to 4 pounds. Hares weigh 3½ pounds for a small snowshoe to 6½ to 10 pounds or so for a large European hare.

Before working with wild rabbits, read about tularemia (see Safety and Health), since these animals are subject to this disease. Be sure to clean and skin rabbits in the field so that they can cool quickly. Since fleas leave an animal as it cools and seek a new, warm host (namely you), don't carry a freshly killed rabbit; instead, hang it in the shade until it has cooled and the fleas have left.

After they are skinned, rabbits and hares can be either quartered or left whole, then cooked or stored in the freezer.

Most rabbits and hares taken by hunters are small. If you do get a large rabbit, chances are it is an older animal that could benefit from marinating before cooking. Use a marinade with an acidic ingredient in it, such as wine, vinegar, or tomato or citrus juice. Marinate it at least overnight; several days will tenderize the meat even more.

Rabbits are more tender and less stringy than hares. The cottontail is by far the most common rabbit on the table. The snowshoe has dark, lean, strongly flavored flesh and could use some marinating to help tenderize it.

Squirrel. Tree squirrels, as the name implies, live in trees; they are the game animals. Ground squirrels, on the other hand, live underground and are not normally hunted for food. Tree squirrels weigh 1 to 2½ pounds, depending on the species.

When skinning a squirrel, remove the glands in the small of the back and under each foreleg. Older squirrels are more difficult to skin.

Treat young squirrels like chicken. Older ones should be marinated and cooked before they are smoked. Place the cooked squirrel in the smoker for up to an hour to achieve a smoke flavor.

Opossum. Opossums are the only marsupials in North America. Their native range includes the eastern United States and California, but they are now found in other parts of the country as well. Opossums weigh 8 to 15 pounds.

Opossums are a popular meat in the South, where they are often treated as suckling pigs and dipped in scalding water so that the hair can be easily scraped off. Most opossums are skinned before they are cooked, however. Remove the red glands in the small of the back and under each foreleg. Also remove excess fat. Soak the animal in salt water overnight, rinse and parboil, then cook using your favorite recipe for pork.

Raccoon. The raccoon is found across most of the United States, except in high mountain or desert areas. This animal lives most often near water, and weighs 10 to 35 pounds.

Since raccoons are fatty, you should remove excess fat after skinning; soak older animals overnight in salt water. Like opossums, these animals benefit from parboiling before they are cooked.

Muskrat. Muskrats are found nationwide wherever there is water. In restaurants, these rodents are often called marsh rabbits.

Muskrats weigh 2 to 4 pounds—about the same as cottontails. They are trapped mainly for their fur; their value as a food source is secondary.

When skinning a muskrat, remove the excess fat, as well as the glands under the front legs and in the small of the back. Soak overnight in salt water to which several tablespoons of vinegar have been added; then cook as you would a squirrel. Older animals benefit from parboiling.

Woodchuck and marmot. Woodchucks are found mainly in the East; marmots, their close relatives, are generally found in the West. Woodchucks are also called groundhogs, and marmots are often called rockchucks. Both animals weigh 5 to 10 pounds.

Skin the animal, remove the glands in the small of the back and under the front arms, and trim away the excess fat. Soak it overnight in salt water. Treat the young ones as young squirrels or chickens; marinate and moist-cook the older, larger ones.

Beaver. Beavers are the largest rodent in North America. These good-sized animals run from 20 to more than 70 pounds, depending on their age and sex.

After removing the pelt, trim away excess fat from the meat. Remove the glands in the small of the back and under the forelegs, and the castor gland pad that lies just under the skin in front of the genitals.

Cut the beaver up, and soak the pieces overnight in salt water to which vinegar has been added. The flesh is dark red and rich, and is often roasted or used in stews.

GAME BIRDS

Game birds—ring-necked pheasant, quail, grouse, turkey, duck, goose, dove, and pigeon—can all be treated approximately the same.

Care. Most hunters dress birds soon after shooting. We recommend this practice, though some people prefer to let the birds first hang, undrawn, for several days to age. They are following the old European custom of letting a bird hang until the body falls away from the head. Some like to hang birds from the head, and some from the feet. Because of the danger of spoilage, do not hang undrawn birds in warm weather or if they are badly shot up.

Still other hunters toss the undressed, unplucked birds into the freezer after several days of hanging. When a bird is to be used, it is dipped into scalding water, which makes plucking easy. Since the bird is frozen solid, it basically stays cold. After the bird is plucked, it is completely thawed, then drawn. One advantage to this method is that the bird is less likely to get freezer burn, since it is protected by its own feathers.

We prefer aging a cleaned, plucked bird in the refrigerator for a few days, but some people leave the birds in the refrigerator seven to ten days before cooking.

You can remove feathers from birds by either skinning or plucking. Skinning birds is faster, but the flavor and protection of the skin is lost. When lean birds such as quail, pigeon, and grouse are skinned, the fat just under the skin is removed. To keep the bird from drying out when it is cooked, you will need to replace the fat.

Birds can be plucked dry, scalded, or dipped in wax. Picking is easiest if done as soon as possible after the bird is killed. Upland birds such as ring-necked pheasant, grouse, and turkey are usually dry-plucked; pull the feathers straight out, a few at a time.

When scalding a bird, dip it up and down in very hot water to loosen the feathers for plucking. When you are finished plucking, you can singe the down off.

Or you can pluck the bird by dipping it in melted wax. First chill the bird, then dip it several times in wax to coat it well. Next, place the bird in the freezer until the wax is hard. The brittle wax can then be cracked and peeled off. The feathers should all come off with the wax.

After skinning or plucking, be sure to check for and remove shotgun pellets. Pull out any feathers that the shot has driven into the flesh. If a bird has a lot of shot, soak it a few hours in a solution of 2 cups salt to 1 gallon of cold water to rid it of any blood that may have collected. Rinse afterward.

Knowing the age of a bird will help you determine how to cook it. Lue learned this lesson the hard way with the first wild goose she cooked. She dutifully stuffed the bird, then roasted it the prescribed amount of time for a bird that size. It looked lovely on the platter. Eating it, however, was like chewing a tennis ball. The next day, she cooked it again in a covered roaster, but it still wasn't tender. Finally, it went into the pressure cooker. The result was a wonderfully tender, flavorful goose. Had Lue known it was an old goose, she would have cooked it properly the first time.

Learn to tell the young from the adults in those species that you hunt basically by looking at the shape of certain feathers and other plumage variations. Consult reference books for guidance.

Cooking. Upland game birds, such as pheasant, chukar partridge, grouse, quail, and dove, are leaner and have a more pronounced flavor than do domestic birds. Unless the bird is young, it may also be less tender than its domestic counterpart, simply because wild birds are more active and often live longer.

Wild waterfowl, such as ducks, geese, and coots, are also leaner than domestic ducks and geese. Wild waterfowl can have a gamy taste, since their diet sometimes includes fish and strongly flavored plants. Bleeding waterfowl in the field helps reduce gamy flavors. You can also soak the birds overnight in milk or in salt water to which several tablespoons of vinegar have been added. After soaking the bird, drain, rinse, then marinate it for hours or even days, using pungent herbs and spices in the marinade mix. Another way to mask gamy flavors is to parboil the birds 15 to 20 minutes in water or wine seasoned with herbs or vegetables.

Young upland game birds and waterfowl are tender and can be treated like chicken. To roast younger birds, push some bacon slices or pork fat under the breast skin, then smoke and cook them by the method of your choice.

Older birds need long, moist cooking. Marinating or brining before smoking will also have a tenderizing effect. Citrus juice, sherry, red wine, ginger, soy sauce, and juniper berries are all good ingredients for brines and marinades for game birds. If you think a bird is going to be rather tough, parboil it before cooking it or put it in a pressure cooker, which works wonders on tough meat. For flavor and eye appeal, roast the bird first to brown it, then put it in the pressure cooker.

If you have skinned the bird, you will need to add fat to replace the natural fat that was under the skin. Baste the bird with oil, butter, or a marinade that contains oil, or place strips of pork or beef fat across the breast.

If you need to transfer the bird to the kitchen oven to finish cooking it after you have smoke-flavored it, you can keep it moist by placing it in a roaster, adding a half-cup of water or wine to the pan, and covering it. Or wrap the meat in aluminum foil and add a little water or wine before folding the foil shut. Cooked, smoked meat can be reheated in a similar manner.

You can give game birds a smoke flavor by smoking them either before or after cooking them, or simply smoke-cooking the birds.

Burgundy Venison Roast

A good hearty wine and any kind of venison complement each other. In this recipe, wine is added to the brine for flavor and to help tenderize the meat.

4 lbs. venison roast, boneless
1 C sugar
1 C salt
1 C burgundy
1 tbsp. Worcestershire sauce
3 bay leaves
2 tsp. black pepper
1 tsp. dry marjoram leaves
1 tsp. chili powder

Tie the roast to keep together, if necessary. Mix the brine ingredients in a nonmetal container, add the meat, then refrigerate up to 48 hours. Turn several times during marination. Drain, pat dry with paper towels, and air-dry for 2 hours. If smoke-cooking, use the water pan filled with water. Cook 4 to 5 hours. Serves 8.

Brandied Moose Roast

Moose is a dry meat, but in this recipe no natural juices are lost; in fact, you add moisture. For a tasty roast, try injecting the meat with a flavored oil mixture, and then marinating it before moist smoke-cooking.

    8 lbs. boneless moose roast
    ½ C brandy
    ½ C olive oil
    ½ tsp. liquid garlic
    2 tbsp. oil
    1 small onion, sliced
    1 small carrot, sliced
    2 garlic cloves, pressed
    1 tbsp. minced parsley
    1 tsp. dry thyme leaves
    3 C red wine
    1 C water
    2 bay leaves

Inject the roast with the brandy, oil, and garlic mixture using a flavor injector. In a fry pan, sauté the onion, carrot, garlic, parsley, and thyme in hot oil until onion is limp. Combine with the remaining marinade ingredients in a large nonmetal bowl. Add the remaining ingredients, including the meat, and marinate 24 to 48 hours, turning several times. Drain, then pat dry with paper towels. Add the marinade to a water pan filled with water. Place the meat on an oiled cooking rack and smoke-cook 7 to 9 hours. Use a thermometer to be sure the meat is cooked enough.

Pumped-up Elk

Injecting a big lean roast with part of the marinade adds moisture and ensures that flavor quickly penetrates the meat.

    8- to 10-lb. elk roast, boneless
    ¾ lb. bacon strips
    1½ C burgundy
    1 tsp. garlic powder
    ¼ C oil
    2 C beef stock
    1 tsp. pepper
    1 tsp. dry basil leaves

Combine 1 cup of the burgundy, garlic, and oil. Use a flavor injector to pump the mixture throughout the meat. Place the meat in a non-metal container. To the remaining liquid, add the beef stock, pepper, and basil and pour over the meat. Cover and refrigerate 1 to 2 days. Preheat an off-set dual chamber smoker to 350 degrees F. (Cooked this way, the meat will take about the same length of time it would in the kitchen oven.) Use a meat thermometer to determine when it is done.

Brandied Venison Flank Steak

One of the secrets to tenderness in flank steak is in the cutting. With a sharp knife, slice the steak thinly across the grain at a long diagonal.

    2 lbs. flank steak, venison, or beef

Barbecue sauce:
    3 C red wine
    ½ C brandy
    ¾ C minced fresh mushrooms
    ¾ C tomato paste
    ¾ C olive oil
    ½ C minced parsley
    6 garlic cloves, pressed
    1 tsp. salt
    ½ tsp. pepper

Bring sauce ingredients to a boil, reduce heat and simmer 15 to 20 minutes, stirring often. In an oblong glass baking dish, pour part of the barbecue sauce in the bottom. Lay the meat in the pan and pour sauce over the top. Cover and let stand about 3 hours. If using a smoke-cooker, use the water pan; smoke-cook approximately 3 hours. Baste the meat once or twice as it is cooking. Serve the remaining sauce with the meat. Serves 4 to 6.

Savory Antelope Roast

The sauce has a distinctive barbecue flavor. Combined with smoked antelope, you get a dish that wins a gold star. Leftover sauce keeps well in the refrigerator and can be served at the table.

    5 lbs. boneless antelope roast, about 2 inches thick

Sauce:

    1 onion
    4 tbsp. olive oil
    1 garlic clove
    ½ C thin sliced celery
    ½ C water
    ¾ C catsup
    ¾ C chili sauce
    2 tbsp. wine vinegar
    2 tbsp. Worcestershire sauce
    1 tsp. prepared horseradish
    1 tsp. prepared mustard
    2 tbsp. lemon juice
    ½ tsp. black pepper
    Several drops Tabasco sauce
    3 tbsp. packed brown sugar
    ½ C dry sherry

Thinly slice onions and garlic, and sauté in hot olive oil in a large fry pan. Mix all remaining ingredients except for meat and wine, and add to onions. Turn down heat and simmer 20 minutes. Add wine, increasing amount until mixture is moderately thick. Simmer another 10 minutes.

Baste the meat well, and place in smoke-cooker for 4 to 5 hours, basting occasionally.

Western Venison

You don't have to live in the West to enjoy this tasty recipe.

    5 lbs. venison roast, boneless
 1½ C beer
   ½ C oil
    1 medium onion, sliced
    2 garlic cloves, pressed
    2 tbsp. lemon juice
    1 tsp. salt
   ½ tsp. pepper
    1 tsp. dry mustard

Combine marinade ingredients and add meat. Cover and refrigerate 48 hours, turning several times to ensure even marination. Smoke-cook about 5 hours. Serves 8 to 10.

Rocky Mountain Sheep Steaks

Wild sheep meat is some of the finest game meat there is. If you have an old animal, this marinade helps tenderize the meat. Be sure not to overcook.

    4 sheep steaks, boneless
   ½ C soy sauce
   ¼ C rice wine
   ½ onion, finely chopped
    2 garlic cloves, pressed
    1 tbsp. grated fresh ginger root
   ¼ tsp. pepper
    1 tsp. liquid smoke

Marinate steaks overnight in the refrigerator, or 3 to 4 hours at room temperature. Cook on hot grill until the meat is done to your preference. Serves 4.

Smoke-Flavored Bear Loin

A good piece of bear meat tastes much like a well-marbled piece of aged beef. We treat bear the same as fresh pork, and cook it until the thermometer reaches 185 degrees F.

5 lbs. pork loin
1 tsp. dry basil leaves
1 tsp. dry oregano leaves
3 garlic cloves, pressed
2 tsp. salt
¼ tsp. coarse ground black pepper

Combine seasoning ingredients and rub well into meat. Preheat electric smokehouse for 15 minutes. Place meat on oiled rack and smoke for 2 hours, using 2 pans of chips. Place meat in range oven preheated to 300 degrees F, and continue cooking until internal temperature of meat reaches 185 degrees F.

Oven-Barbecued Bear

Try this recipe for any red meat, big or small game animals.

> 3 to 4 lbs. bear tenderloin
> 2 onions, sliced

Barbecue sauce:
> 1 C catsup
> ½ tsp. Tabasco sauce
> ⅓ tsp. chili powder
> 1 C water
> 1 tsp. prepared mustard
> 2 to 3 tbsp. packed brown sugar
> ½ to 1 tsp. liquid smoke

Preheat the oven to 350 degrees F. Cut the loin into half-inch slices; place in a baking pan and cook in the oven for half an hour. Combine all sauce ingredients in a saucepan and simmer gently. When the half hour is up, strain off excess fat from the pan. Layer onion slices on top of the meat, pour the sauce over the meat and onions, cover, and bake about 1 hour. Uncover the last 15 minutes to allow the sauce to thicken. Serves 6.

Teriyaki Kabobs

If you prefer, you can use this recipe to marinate the meat as a roast. Either way, it has delicious flavor.

2½ to 3 lbs. boneless bear, javelina, or wild boar

Marinade:
> 1 C soy sauce
> ⅓ C dry sherry
> 4 tbsp. brown sugar
> 1 tbsp. grated fresh ginger root
> 1 tbsp. dry minced onion
> 1 garlic clove, pressed
>
> Canned pineapple chunks
> Fresh mushrooms

Cut the meat into 1-inch cubes. In a nonmetal bowl, mix together the marinade ingredients. Add the meat cubes and marinate at least 3 hours at room temperature. Thread the meat on skewers, leaving a space between each piece of meat. Set the water pan in place. Place the kabobs on the oiled cooking rack. Smoke-cook 3 to 3½ hours. Alternate the mushrooms and pineapple on separate skewers. Brush them with the marinade and add them to the smoke-cooker the last 2 hours of cooking. Heat the remaining marinade to serve at the table. Serves 6 to 8.

Soused Rabbit

Some people prefer rabbit to chicken because they feel rabbit has more flavor. You can prepare rabbit using almost any chicken recipe.

     2 rabbits, dressed and cut up
     ½ C dry vermouth
     ¼ C burgundy
     ½ C oil
     1 tsp. liquid smoke
     1 tsp. tarragon
     1 tsp. seasoned salt
     2 cloves garlic, pressed
     2 tbsp. minced parsley
     1 tsp. minced onion
     ⅛ tsp. pepper
        Butter for basting

     Combine all marinade ingredients. Add the rabbit and let marinate for several hours. Add soaked wood chips or chunks to readied briquettes in a barbecue unit. Grill the rabbit on low setting for about 45 minutes, basting frequently with butter. Serves 4 to 6.

Rabbit in Tomato Sauce

The light, fine-grained flesh of the rabbit is quite lean and needs either a sauce or frequent basting to keep it from drying out. This is a good dish if you are cooking an older rabbit. If you like, you can add liquid smoke to the recipe and bake the rabbit in the oven.

3 lbs. rabbit, cut up
1 C dry vermouth
3 garlic cloves, pressed
  Oil

Sauce:

3 garlic cloves, pressed
1 onion, chopped
2 tbsp. oil
¼ C tomato puree
1 C chicken broth
½ C fine bread crumbs
2 tbsp. dry vermouth
1 tsp. salt
⅛ tsp. pepper
¼ tsp. dry thyme leaves

Combine the vermouth and garlic and marinate the rabbit overnight. If the dish is smoke-cooked, save the marinade to add to the water pan of the smoke-cooker. Remove the rabbit from the marinade, pat dry, and brown the meat on all sides in hot oil. After browning, transfer the meat to a casserole. In the meantime, prepare the sauce by sautéing the garlic and onion in hot oil. Add the remaining ingredients and simmer until the sauce thickens slightly. Pour the sauce over the rabbit and put on the cooking rack of a gas smoke-cooker, with the water pan in place. Cook 3 to 4 hours. A young, tender rabbit will take about an hour less.

Squirrel Picante

Squirrels are the second most popular small game, and many people think they are the tastiest.

       2 large squirrels, dressed and cut up
       1 C tomato or V-8 juice
     ¼ C oil
     ½ onion, chopped
       2 garlic cloves, pressed
          Juice of 1 lemon
       2 tbsp. Worcestershire sauce
     ½ tsp. salt
     ¼ tsp. pepper
    1½ tsp. cumin seed, crushed

Combine all the marinade ingredients, mix well, add the rabbit, and refrigerate overnight. Turn several times. When ready to cook, pour the remaining marinade in a water pan filled with water. Place the meat on the oiled cooking rack and smoke-cook 2½ to 3 hours. Serves approximately 4.

Italian Squirrel

Take 2 dressed, cut-up squirrels and marinate overnight in 1 cup of prepared Italian salad dressing. Fill the water pan with water. Add several sprigs of fresh oregano or basil. Place the meat on the oiled cooking rack and smoke-cook for 2½ to 3 hours. Serves approximately 4.

Smoked Stuffed Pheasant

Smoke 2 pheasants. Start with the following brine:

¼ C water
¼ C soy sauce
¼ C dry white wine
¼ C brown sugar
½ tsp. onion powder
½ tsp. garlic powder
½ tsp. ground ginger

Place cleaned birds in cold brine for 6 hours. Rinse, pat dry, and let air-dry for 1 hour. Smoke in electric smokehouse, with 2 panfuls of wood chips, for 2 to 4 hours.

While the pheasants are smoking, prepare the following stuffing:

⅓ C butter or margarine
¼ C minced onion
¼ C minced celery
1 tsp. dried thyme
½ tsp. salt
⅛ tsp. pepper
1⅓ C dry bread crumbs
⅔ C chopped hazelnuts
Flour, salt, and pepper
¼ C butter or margarine
1½ C hot water
⅓ C dry vermouth
1 tsp. sugar

Preheat oven to 350 degrees F. In a large frying pan, melt ⅓ C butter; sauté onion and celery. Add bread crumbs, nuts, salt, pepper, and thyme, and mix lightly. Remove pheasants from the smoker, fill the cavities with stuffing, and skewer or sew shut. Sprinkle lightly with salt and pepper, and rub flour over the skin. Melt the remaining butter, and brown each bird on all sides. Transfer to a roasting pan. Dissolve sugar in water; add this mixture and vermouth to the pan. Cover and bake for 1 hour. Serves 6. (Recipe from Luhr Jensen and Sons, Inc.)

Smoked Grouse

With or without a stuffing, smoked grouse makes a memorable meal. Stuffing the cavity with apple, celery, and onion allows the flavors to permeate the meat from the inside during smoking.

    1 or 2 dressed pheasants
    2 C burgundy
      Water
    2 garlic cloves
    1 onion, sliced
    2 bay leaves, crumbled
    ¼ C olive oil
    2 tsp. salt
    1 tsp. pepper
    2 tsp. crushed marjoram leaves
      Half an apple
      Rib of celery
      Half an onion

   Place birds in nonmetal container. Add wine with enough cold water to cover pheasants. Add garlic, onion, and bay leaves. Cover and refrigerate 18 to 24 hours. Remove birds and pat dry with paper towels. Rub pheasants with olive oil, then sprinkle well with salt, pepper, and marjoram. Stuff the cavity with apple, celery, and onion. If using a smoke-cooker, put the water pan in place, pour in marinade, and fill with water. Smoke-cook about 3 hours.

Glazed Stuffed Duck

If you use wild ducks for this recipe, you can prevent the birds from drying out by laying pork fat strips across the breast, or by pushing the fat under the breast skin.

     2 wild ducks or 1 5-lb. domestic duck
        Salt and pepper
    ½ onion, cut in half
        Parsley sprigs
     3 to 4 garlic cloves, quartered
    ½ orange, cut in half

Glaze:
    ⅓ C soy sauce
     2 tbsp. honey
     2 tbsp. lemon juice
    ⅛ tsp. garlic powder

Rinse bird, drain, and pat dry. Sprinkle the cavity with salt and pepper. Stuff the cavity with the onion, parsley, garlic, and orange. Tie the tail and legs together; lock the wings behind the back. Skewer the neck skin over the back. Combine and heat glaze ingredients. Brush the entire duck with the glaze. Add herbs and garlic cloves to the water pan. Place the duck on the oiled cooking rack. Cover and smoke-cook 4 to 5 hours. Brush occasionally with glaze. Serves 6.

Smoked Soy-Sauced Breast of Duck

Although many people prefer duck meat rare, if you prefer your duck breast well done, this recipe may be for you.

    Breasts of 2 ducks
¼ C flour
¼ tsp. pepper
¼ tsp. garlic powder
2 tbsp. butter
    Pineapple juice, plus enough water to make 1 cup
2 tbsp. soy sauce
1 tsp. chicken bouillon granules
1 onion, sliced
1 bell pepper, cut into strips
1 8-oz. can pineapple chunks, drained (reserve juice)
¾ C almonds

Remove the skin from the duck breasts. Rub lightly with oil and smoke for about 45 minutes. Combine the flour, pepper, and garlic powder and rub into the duck. Brown the meat in butter in a Dutch oven or heavy fry pan. Add pineapple juice and water, soy sauce, and bouillon. Cover, bring to a boil, reduce heat to simmer, and cook about 15 minutes. Add onion, bell pepper, pineapple, and almonds. Cover and simmer another 15 minutes, or until meat is tender. Adjust seasonings. Liquids may be thickened by adding a mixture of cornstarch and water, if desired. Serves 4.

Stuffed Small Birds

A platter of smoked birds is a delight to both the eye and the palate. These stuffed birds offer a scrumptious combination of flavors, both inside and out.

      4 small birds such as quail or Cornish game hens
      3 tbsp. soy sauce
      3 tbsp. brandy
      1 tbsp. packed brown sugar
      1 tsp. salt
    ¼ tsp. pepper
      1 medium onion, chopped
      4 gizzards, sliced
      3 tbsp. butter or margarine
      2 C diced bread
      3 shrimp, chopped
      6 water chestnuts, sliced
      1 C milk
      1 tsp. salt
    ¼ tsp. pepper
         Oil

Combine the soy sauce, brandy, brown sugar, salt, and pepper, and marinate the cleaned birds in this mixture for an hour. Spoon the mixture into the cavity several times. Sauté the onion and gizzards in 1 tablespoon of the butter. Add remaining butter, and stir in the bread, shrimp, water chestnuts, milk, salt, and pepper. Stuff the birds with this mixture and skewer shut. Tie the legs together. Brush the outside of the birds with oil and hot-smoke for 1½ hours. Brush with oil once during cooking. Allow 1 or 2 birds per person, depending on the size of the birds.

Smoke-Flavored Chinese Duck or Goose

For a deliciously flavored, browned bird, brine a duck or a domestic or wild goose overnight in the following marinade:

- 1½ C water
- 1 C soy sauce
- ½ C pineapple juice
- ½ C dry sherry
- ¼ C sugar
- ¼ C salt
- 1 tsp. onion powder
- 2 garlic cloves, pressed
- 2 tbsp. grated fresh ginger root

Combine the marinade ingredients, and soak the bird overnight. Remove the bird from the brine and pat dry. Let air-dry for several hours to acquire a glaze. Place the bird on oiled racks in a preheated electric smokehouse. Smoke 2½ to 3 hours, using 2 pans of chips. To finish cooking, transfer to a range oven preheated to 300 degrees F.

❖

Fish
and
Shellfish

❖

Smoked fish is fish that has been brined, air-dried, then smoked over hardwood. The difference between true smoked fish and fish cooked on a barbecue grill or smoke-cooked in a moist, slow-cooking unit is that the former is mainly smoked, and the latter is mainly cooked.

Most fresh and saltwater fish and shellfish can be smoked. Fish can be hot-smoked or cold-smoked. Fish that is cold-smoked is usually not cooked at all, though some cooking may occur in the upper temperature ranges. Hot-smoked fish may be cooked anywhere from slightly to completely.

Whether it is cold- or hot-smoked, the fish is almost always cured by either a dry cure or a brine before smoking. Fish that is hot-smoked does not have to be brined first, but the flavor is much improved if it is.

The amount of moisture left in the finished product depends on your personal preference. Most smoked fish must be refrigerated or frozen unless it has been dried enough to prevent spoilage.

There are many types of fish that are smoked or treated in some way. For example, Indian-cured fish is brined and then cold-smoked for up to two weeks; the term also refers to strips of salted or unsalted fish that have been hung outside on racks to dry. Either method results in a very dry product that is often called fish jerky.

In the United States, kippered fish refers to steaks, fillets, or chunks put in a mild brine, then hot-smoked. European-style kippered fish is placed in a stronger brine, smoked, then baked or hot-smoked.

Lox is fatty fish, such as salmon, that has been cold-smoked. It can be either salty or mild. Seelachs is like fake smoked salmon, and is often made by slicing lightly smoked, white-fleshed fish and dyeing it to resemble salmon. Gravlax, a Swedish specialty, is raw salmon cured in salt, sugar, and dill and sliced paper-thin. One particular method of preparing cold-smoked salmon is called Scotch smoked salmon, Nova Scotia smoked salmon, Danish smoked salmon, or other names, depending on the region of the country or part of the world. Squaw candy is a term sometimes used for thin strips of fish cured in a salt and sugar brine before they are hot-smoked.

Care. Fish and shellfish are delicate, so handle with care. Absolute freshness is important regardless of how the fish is prepared.

Sometimes it's difficult to get really fresh fish from the store. If you can find a dependable market that sells fresh fish, take advantage of it. Otherwise, frozen fish may be your best bet. Fish that is frozen on the boat soon after it is caught will be fresher than so-called fresh fish that sat many hours before it was processed on shore.

When purchasing fish from the market, you should look for several things:

- Gills should be bright red and have a clear mucus. Don't select fish with gray or brownish gills and cloudy mucus.
- Eyes should be bright and clean, not dull and sunken.
- Flesh should be firm and should not leave finger impressions when lightly pressed. The flesh should be firmly attached to the bones.
- The vent should be pink, not gray or brownish.
- Scales should be bright, shiny, and firmly attached.
- Fillets and steaks should look moist and firm, including the edges.
- Truly fresh fish does not smell fishy.
- Packaged frozen fish should be free of a lot of ice crystals. Packages should be well sealed.

When harvesting your own fish, remember that fish are extremely perishable. Keep it clean, cool, and dry. If you care for your fish properly, you will be rewarded with an excellent meal. But if the fish has deteriorated, the smoking process won't reverse the damage.

According to the University of Alaska's Marine Advisory Program, there are five main reasons for poor quality in fish: bruising, rancidity or oxidation, belly burn, spoilage by enzymes and bacteria, and dehydration.

Some experts suggested stunning freshly caught fish so that they don't flop around and become bruised. Bruising makes fish less edible, by causing blood to seep into the flesh. Tossing a dead, uncleaned fish in the bottom of the boat in the hot sun also leads to deterioration.

Belly burn is caused by failure to clean fish quickly; dress fish as soon as possible to prevent digestive enzymes from burning through the stomach. The enzymes and bacteria within a fish go to work upon its death, thus diminishing the flavor as well as the storage life of the fish.

If a fish is gaffed, it should be hooked under the gills or in the head. Handle large fish by the head instead of the tail; lifting large fish by the tail can break the spine, which in turn can pull the flesh away from the bone. Bleed fish, especially large species, since blood contaminates the flesh. Always store fish in a well-drained area. Last but not least, keep the fish as cold as possible. (For more on this subject, write to MAP, 2221 E. Northern Lights Blvd., Suite 220, Anchorage, AK 99508.)

If you are smoking whole small fish or fish sections, such as steaks and fillets, you may need to remove the skin. Scrape the scales off and remove the slime by rinsing the fish in a vinegar solution of one part vinegar to four parts water and scrubbing it with a brush.

Wash the body cavity well; a toothbrush does a good job of cleaning along the backbone. Remove the head and the fins, including the tail, from large fish. If you are hanging large fillets to be smoked, leave the collarbone attached to provide a solid place from which to hang the fish.

Fillet the fish or cut steaks about 1 inch thick, then cut each steak in half at the backbone. To leach blood from the fish and to firm it up a bit, place the fish in a cold saline solution of 1 cup pickling salt to 1 gallon of water. Let it stand for one hour. Remove the fish, rinse it well to remove excess salt, and blot it lightly.

Keep the fish refrigerated until it is cured. If you must temporarily store fish without refrigeration or ice, clean and wash it, then sprinkle the cavity generously with a mixture of 1 cup of salt and 1 tablespoon of pepper. Use 4 tablespoons of this mixture for every pound of fish. Place the fish in a container where the air can circulate, and cover it with damp burlap. Rinse the fish well when you are ready to use it. This procedure should keep the fish in good shape up to 24 hours in cool weather.

Curing. Fish can be cured in a heavily salted cure and smoked until it is completely dry. Most people find heavily salted, dried fish unpalatable, however. Furthermore, this method of curing is no longer necessary, thanks to refrigeration.

Nevertheless, a certain amount of salt is required to produce tasty smoked fish that is safe to eat, especially when fish are cold-smoked. If fish is cured with a brine, the recommended minimum is 2 cups of salt to 1 gallon of water, or approximately 60 degrees on a salinometer. Some experts recommend between 70 and 90 degrees; a 90-degree solution is about 3⅔ cups of salt to 1 gallon of water. When measuring salt, use either a scale or a measuring cup for dry measure. A measuring cup holding 8 fluid ounces will hold 12 ounces of salt.

In some fish recipes, the salt content is below the recommended minimum, which means the fish will absorb more liquid and take more time to dry. When a less salty fish is desired, experts usually recommend curing the fish in the standard brine for a shorter time, rather than using a brine containing less salt. Nevertheless, we have included recipes using a weaker brine, since we personally like the results. If you would prefer more salt in a particular brine, then by all means add it.

After preparing the brine, add the fish and weight it under a large plate, right side up to keep an air pocket from forming, and adding a clean weight to the top.

Always keep the brine and fish cold. If the containers are too large to fit in the refrigerator, put ice in plastic bags and place the sealed bags inside the brine crock. Be sure the bags are well sealed and don't have holes; otherwise the brine will be diluted.

Brining time depends on many variables and can range from about a half an hour to many hours or even days. Fish that is lean, skinless, or cut in small or thin pieces requires less brining time than fish that is oily, has skin, or is cut in large, thick pieces. Thawed frozen fish absorbs salt more quickly than fresh fish. The fresher the fish, the longer the curing time needed. The longer the cure, the higher the salt content in the cured fish.

To estimate brining time, consider the size of the individual pieces of fish, not the total weight. Five pounds of small fillets will weigh as much as one 5-pound piece, but the smaller pieces require less brining time.

After brining, remove the fish and follow the directions for each brine. Some recipes specify rinsing; others advise against it. Pat the fish lightly with paper towels, then air-dry.

Instead of brining fish, you can use a dry cure. One way is to score thick pieces of fish lengthwise and rub the cure mixture into the cuts. Lay the fish in a nonmetallic or stainless steel pan and refrigerate it overnight. Remove the fish from the refrigerator, rinse it in running water, pat dry, then air-dry.

For more information, see Preparing Foods for Smoking.

Drying. After fish is cured, it needs to dry long enough to acquire a pellicle, that is, a thin glaze that forms on the outside of the fish. The pellicle aids in the development of flavor and color as the fish is smoking. It also helps keep in the juices and retain the firm texture and shape of the fish as it is being smoked.

The fish can be dried indoors, or outdoors in the shade, but not in the sun. A cool breeze is helpful, but if there is none, you can speed up the process by setting up a fan on low speed. Drying can take one to several hours, depending on the fish and the weather. You can also dry fish by hanging it or draping it across racks in the smokehouse, or placing it on the racks that go into the electric smokehouses. If you have metal racks, oil them first to prevent the fish from sticking.

Smoking. How the fish is put in the smoker depends on the unit itself and whether the fish is whole or cut up. Whole fish are frequently hung by S hooks or on small dowels pushed through the gill slits. If you are planning to hang large fillets, leave the collarbone on so that the rods can be pushed through the fillets, under the collarbone. Fillets can be draped across rods, but the ends hanging down should not touch. Fillets with the skin on should be laid on racks with the skin side down. Prop whole and split fish open so that smoke can penetrate evenly. You can prop open the cavity of small whole fish using short pieces of wood, such as wooden skewers or Popsicle sticks broken to the proper length.

Although oily fish will remain moist because of their natural oils, lean fish may need occasional basting during the smoking process. You can also brush fish lightly with oil after smoking.

As estimated smoking time nears the end, sample the fish to see whether it is as dry as you like. Smaller pieces take less time than larger ones, and in some smoker units, the fish on the bottom racks will be ready before the pieces on the top racks. Remove those that are done, and leave the others a little longer. A full smokehouse or oven will take longer than one that is partially full.

Hot-smoking. The fish has been brined, dry-cured, or marinated, then air-dried and placed in a preheated smoker. The temperature range of hot-smoking will cook the fish at least partially while it is drying. A little experience will soon teach you approximately how many hours you'll need to reach the stage of dryness you like for the thickness of the fish you are smoking. As soon as the fish has cooled, wrap it loosely in wax paper and store it in the refrigerator. It will keep well in the refrigerator one to three weeks, depending upon how dry it is. Always remember that smoked fish is perishable.

Our favorite way to hot-smoke fish is in our electric smokehouse because the unit is designed to raise the internal temperature of the food to 165 degrees F.

Smoke according to the directions supplied with the smoke oven, smokehouse, barbecue, or whatever type of unit you have. If you are using an electric smokehouse, you will need several pans of wood chips during the first few hours of smoking. (Smoke doesn't have to be applied during the entire drying time.) Generally, the fish will be ready in 5 to 12 hours, depending on the fish, the unit used, personal preferences, and the weather. Let cool, then wrap and refrigerate the food.

Cold-smoking. Prepare the fish as you would for hot-smoking, using a dry cure or brine. In this case, however, you must add curing salts, unless the cure already has a high salt content.

Preheat the smokehouse while the fish is drying. The temperature inside the smokehouse should be low (about 70 degrees F), with a light smoke. After the fish has been smoked approximately 12 hours, a heavier smoke can be applied. Smoking time can take from 24 hours to two weeks, depending on the type and size of fish, and how dry you want it. The longer the smoking time, the longer the fish will keep.

There are other approaches to cold-smoking fish. For example, fish can be placed in a smokehouse preheated to 75 to 85 degrees F and smoked from one day to two weeks. Fish can also be lightly smoked for about 8 hours at 80 to 90 degrees F, then densely smoked another 4 hours as you gradually increase the temperature to 130 to 150 degrees F. Hold the smokehouse temperature for another 2 or 3 hours, or until the fish turns a shiny brown.

Cold-smoking the fish before hot-smoking it will give the hot-smoked fish a stronger flavor.

To store cold-smoked fish, wrap each piece in plastic wrap and foil, then refrigerate or freeze it.

Fish can also be dried in a dehydrator or oven for 12 to 14 hours at 140 to 160 degrees F. If you want a smoke flavor, add liquid smoke to the brine. When using an oven, leave the door slightly ajar to allow moisture to escape.

Obviously, cold-smoking fish is more involved than hot-smoking, and requires a different type of unit. If you are new to smoking, we suggest you begin with a unit that hot-smokes and is easy to use. That way, you can become acquainted with cures and marinades, the general smoking process, and your personal preferences. Then if you wish to learn the finer points of smoking, you can build or buy a cold-smoking unit.

Smoking fish is not an exact science. You will need to experiment to find out what you like and what works best in your type of smokehouse. Try different cures and flavoring ingredients, woods, smoking methods and times, and types or cuts of fish. Keep notes about the results that so you can duplicate those you liked the best.

Cooking. Fish cooks quickly and easily, and will continue to cook to some degree even after it is removed from the heat source. Fish is edible when the internal temperature reaches 140 degrees F. At 150 degrees F, the tissue begins to break down, allowing juices and flavor to escape. Fish that is overcooked will lose moisture and flavor and become dry and tough or rubbery.

SHELLFISH

Shellfish are tasty, high in protein, and low in calories. For those people who like both shellfish and smoke flavor, the combination is heavenly.

Shellfish are highly perishable, so purchase from a reliable market or harvest them yourself. If any shellfish smells the least bit old or fishy, don't buy it. Ideally, you should eat what you purchase or harvest the same day. Shrimp doesn't stay fresh very long; fresh clams and oysters can be kept on ice in the refrigerator for several days.

If you want to harvest your own shellfish, check with local bait and tackle shops for the best places to go and ask about safety warnings. Some shellfish, such as scallops, clams, oysters, and mussels, are filter-feeders. They siphon seawater to extract microscopic plankton, some of which can cause paralytic shellfish poisoning to mammals. Most harvesting areas are monitored by authorities and posted if there is any danger.

Crabs. Fresh crabs are available in most supermarkets whole, or as lump meat, flakes, a mixture of lumps and flakes, or legs. Crab can also be purchased canned or frozen. In addition, there is an imitation crab, which is made from fish and flavored with the juices from crab.

Shrimp. Shrimp have a distinctive flavor and tender, juicy meat that is even more delectable when smoked. They can be purchased fresh, peeled or unpeeled, veined or deveined, and frozen, canned, or dried. Fresh shrimp are extremely perishable and should always be kept refrigerated.

Lobster. Lobster is often available live, in tanks, at markets. Lobster tails, lumps, and flakes are available fresh, frozen, or canned. As with crab, there is imitation lobster made from fish and flavored with lobster juice. Even when using high-priced lobster, you don't need a lot; added to a favorite seafood dish, a little smoked lobster goes a long way. The mild, delicate flavor of lobster needs only a light smoking.

Clams. Clam digging is an inexpensive, popular family sport in many coastal areas. Fresh clams, whole or shucked, can also be purchased in many markets, or they can be purchased canned in various forms.

Fresh clams should be cleaned as soon as possible. Shucking is easier if the clams are dipped in boiling water for up to one minute. Clams can be smoked in the shell, shelled, or minced, after being combined with other foods.

Mussels. Harvesting mussels is another popular sport in some coastal areas. Mussels used to be considered a poor man's food, but they are now more popular and sometimes found in markets. Mussel flesh is orange and rich in flavor. Treat mussels as you would clams. Smoking adds to their flavor.

Oysters. Many coastal residents once harvested their own oysters, but today most of these shellfish are found in commercial oyster beds that are closed to public harvesting. Oysters can be purchased live in the shell or shucked, fresh or frozen. They also come in cans in whole, minced, or smoked form.

Scallops. These bivalves are usually available at the market already shucked. Although they will keep on ice for up to two days, it is a good idea to eat them as soon as they are purchased.

Garden in a Fish

This dish is especially attractive at the table. Serve it on a platter and garnish with greens, cherry tomatoes or carrot curls, and black olives.

> Whole cleaned fish, about 5 lbs.
> 2 C chopped vegetables such as carrots, onions, zucchini, green bell pepper, and red bell pepper
> ¼ C butter or margarine
> 2 tbsp. minced fresh coriander
> 1 tsp. salt
> ½ tsp. black pepper
> Juice of 1 lemon

Place the fish in Bay Leaf Brine for Fish (page 38) for 4 hours. Rinse well, pat dry, then air-dry until glaze forms on the skin.

Sauté the vegetables and herbs in butter. Add the salt, pepper, and lemon juice. Stuff the cavity with the mix, and skewer closed. Put the water pan in place and fill with water. Add some herbs to the water, if desired. Place the fish on an oiled cooking rack and smoke-cook about 3 hours. Serves approximately 8.

Swordfish Imperial

Although swordfish is expensive, this recipe makes it worth the price. Its firm, lean flesh is a special treat when smoke-cooked.

> 2 lbs. swordfish
> ¾ C olive oil
> ⅓ C lemon juice
> 1 bay leaf, broken
> Several drops hot pepper sauce

Mix marinade ingredients in a nonmetallic bowl. Add the fish and marinate 30 to 60 minutes at room temperature. Pour the marinade in the water pan and add water until pan is nearly full. Place the fish on the oiled cooking rack. Cover and smoke-cook for about 2 hours. Serves 4 to 6.

Italian Steelhead

The flavor of most fish is enhanced by this type of marinade. Since it is oily, it is also good for lean fish.

2 lbs. steelhead steaks or fillets
2 C Italian salad dressing
2 tbsp. dry white wine
¼ tsp. black pepper

Combine the marinade ingredients in a nonmetallic bowl. Marinate the fish for 30 minutes. Put the water pan in place, fill with water, and add some herbs. Smoke-cook 2 to 3 hours or until the fish is done. Serves 4 to 6.

Tuna Smoke

If you've never tried fresh tuna, you are in for a treat. It is meaty, firm, and delicious.

4 fresh tuna steaks
1 8-oz. can tomato sauce
1 small onion, chopped
1 garlic clove, pressed
¼ C minced green bell pepper
3 tbsp. lemon juice
1 tsp. celery seed
1 tbsp. sugar

Combine marinade ingredients and marinate fish for approximately 1 hour. Set the water pan in place, fill with water, and add some herbs. Place the fish on an oiled grill and smoke-cook 2 to 3 hours, or until the fish is done. Spoon more sauce over the fish once while cooking. Serve the remaining sauce at the table. Serves 4.

Halibut with Basil

The white, meaty, lean flesh of the halibut tastes great no matter how it is prepared. For a more pronounced smoke flavor, add a bit of liquid smoke.

    4 ³⁄₄- to 1-inch thick halibut steaks
    ¼ C melted butter or oil
       Juice of 1 lemon
       Seasoned salt
       Crushed dry basil leaves, or chopped fresh leaves

Place steaks in an aluminum foil pan. Combine the butter and lemon, and drizzle half the mixture over the fish; sprinkle with seasoned salt. Turn and repeat. Set the water pan in place and fill with hot water. Put the fish on the cooking grill, cover, and smoke-cook about 3 hours, or until fish just flakes when checked with a fork. Sprinkle with crushed basil leaves. Serves 4.

Smoked Whole Sea Bass

Use this recipe for any large whole fish to be smoke-cooked.

   1   whole fish, about 10 lbs.
 ¼   C lemon juice
 ¼   C dry vermouth
   1   tbsp. Worcestershire sauce
   1   tsp. crushed dry basil
 ½   tsp. crushed dry oregano
 ¼   tsp. garlic powder
 ½   tsp. salt
   1   onion, thinly sliced
   1   lemon, thinly sliced
        Oil

Combine lemon juice, vermouth, sauce, herbs, and salt. Sprinkle the mixture in the fish cavity, reserving a small amount. Lay half the onion and lemon slices in the cavity. Brush the outside of the fish with oil, then lay the remaining half of onion and lemon slices on top. Sprinkle with the remaining herb-salt mixture. Put the water pan in place and fill. Place the fish on the oiled cooking grill, and drizzle the remaining lemon mixture over the top, letting any excess drip into the water pan below. Smoke-cook 3 to 4 hours, or until the fish flakes when tested with a fork.

Simple Salmon

This recipe is simple but dramatic. The rich flavors of salmon are complemented by the smoke and the lemon and onion flavors. Serve this dish either hot or cold, with a choice of sauces.

> 6- to 7-lb. whole salmon, cleaned
> Salt
> Pepper
> Onion slices
> Lemon slices
> Dill weed

Wash the fish and pat dry. Salt and pepper the cavity. Lay lemon and onion slices in the cavity. Lay some pieces of dill weed on top of the slices. Put the water pan in place, fill, and add some dill to the water. Place fish on oiled cooking rack. Cover and smoke-cook 2 hours, or until fish flakes when tested with a fork.

Sweet and Smoky Fish Fillets

Herbs and brown sugar combine to make an excellent flavoring for most fish.

> 3 lbs. fillets of any large fish
> ¼ C brown sugar
> ¼ C oil
> 1 tsp. dry crushed herbs such as thyme or marjoram

Use a dry cure, or brine the fish for 4 hours. After brining, rinse well, pat dry, and air-dry for 1 hour. Combine brown sugar, oil and herbs, and rub the mixture over the entire fish. Put the water pan in place, fill with water, and add several sprigs of fresh herbs or 1 tablespoon of dry herbs. Place the fish on an oiled cooking rack, skin side down, and smoke-cook approximately 2 hours. Serves 5 to 6.

Smoked Salmon Fingers

For tasty hors d'oeuvres, try this recipe.

Slice a salmon fillet into fingersize pieces. Marinate in a mixture of lemon juice, olive oil, and dill weed for half an hour. Place on a perforated aluminum foil pan and smoke 30 to 45 minutes, or until done to your taste.

Stuffed Smoked Clams

This dish is a special hors d'oeuvre. To serve it as a main meal, figure 8 clams per person.

     12 large fresh clams
      4 tbsp. butter or margarine
      1 onion, minced
    ¼ C minced green bell pepper
    ½ tsp. dry marjoram leaves, crushed
    ½ tsp. salt
         Several dashes hot pepper sauce
      1 C fine dry bread crumbs
    ¼ C cream
         Grated fresh Parmesan cheese

Scrub clams and place in 1 quart of boiling water. Cover and simmer for 6 minutes, or until shells just open. Remove and cool. Remove clams from shell, reserving shells. Pour off any juice and save. Chop clams. In a fry pan, melt butter and sauté onion, bell pepper, and marjoram. Add bread crumbs, and cook another several minutes. Fill shells with the mixture. Pour a little cream over each and top off with Parmesan cheese. Put on a perforated foil tray and place in a preheated smokehouse for 30 minutes, using ½ a pan of chips during the process. Serves 4 as an appetizer.

Smoke-Cooked Shrimp

Garlic and thyme are the perfect complement to smoked shrimp.

    1 lb. peeled, deveined shrimp
    ¼ C butter, melted
    2 garlic cloves, pressed
    ½ tsp. salt
    ¼ tsp. crushed thyme
      Paprika

Put the water pan in place and fill about ⅔ full of hot water. Place shrimp in a shallow heavy-duty aluminum tray and set on cooking grill. Combine the butter, garlic, salt, and thyme, and drizzle over shrimp. Smoke-cook about 1 hour, or until shrimp are firm and pink. Sprinkle with paprika.

Brined Smoked Shrimp

These shrimp are a delicious snack. They can also be used in casseroles or mixed into dips and spreads.

Use cooked shrimp. If starting with raw shrimp, cook first in a seasoned bouillon for 5 minutes; drain and pat dry. Submerge the cooked shrimp in a basic brine of water, salt, and sugar (see Preparing Foods for Smoking) for 2 hours. Rinse and pat dry. Lay the shrimp on paper towels and air-dry for 45 minutes. Place them on an oiled aluminum tray poked with holes, or on an oiled screen. Use 2 pans full of dry wood chips, and smoke 2 hours in an electric smokehouse.

Smoked Shellfish

There are various ways to smoke shellfish. In addition, they can be smoked by species or as a group.

Shrimp. Peel and devein.

Scallops. Rinse.

Oysters, mussels, or clams. Wash well and steam 5 minutes or until the shells open. Discard any that do not open.

Place on a foil tray and smoke at 250 degrees F for 30 to 45 minutes. Serve with lemon-parsley butter.

Oysters, clams, mussels, and scallops in the shell. Steam until they open. Discard any that do not open. Place a pan under the shellfish to catch the liquid, if desired. If oysters are shucked, dip them in boiling water until the gills curl. Soak the shellfish in a brine from 30 to 45 minutes. Rinse, place on an oiled screen or aluminum foil pan with the bottom pierced, and set aside until dry. Smoke 2 hours in an electric smokehouse using 2 pans full of chips.

Prawns, shrimp, or crayfish. Peel and precook in seasoned water for 5 minutes. Cook, then place in a brine for 2 hours. Rinse and place on an oiled screen or aluminum foil pan with the bottom pierced. Air-dry. Smoke 2 hours in an electric smokehouse using 2 pans full of chips.

Shellfish with Dipping Sauce

Smoked shellfish, served on a big platter with a bowl of dipping sauce, has special appeal.

Lobster, crab, or shrimp in the shell. Crack shells lightly to allow the smoke to get inside. If using a smoke-cooker, add 1 cup of wine and several sprigs of fresh herbs to the water pan. Place lobster or crab on the oiled cooking grill; place shrimp on a perforated aluminum tray. Smoke-cook for 30 minutes to 1 hour.

Dip for shellfish. Combine and heat ¼ C peanut oil, 2 pressed garlic cloves, and 1 tablespoon grated fresh ginger root.

Smoked Oysters

Try this simple idea for oysters on your guests while they are waiting for dinner.

Place shucked and cleaned oysters in an aluminum foil pan. Brush with a mixture of lemon juice and melted butter. Smoke 1 to 2 hours, or until firm but not rubbery.

Smoked Lobster Tails

These lightly smoked lobster tails make an elegant supper or buffet dish.

Remove membrane from underside of lobster tails. To prevent curling, bend tail backward until shell is cracked. Brush each tail with melted butter. Use water pan and fill ⅔ full. Smoke-cook 1 hour. Season with melted butter and fresh lemon juice.

Variety Meats

The organ meats, such as liver, heart, tripe, and kidneys, can be brined or marinated, then smoked. Tongue is another favorite smoked meat.

For liver and heart, you might want to try the same brines and marinades that are suggested for venison and beef dishes. Milder brines and marinades often work well for poultry and game bird hearts, livers, and gizzards. Whether you are looking for a mild or strong seasoning, or something in between, most brines or marinades can be used for any of the organ meats.

Wine with a Heart

To many hunters, the heart and liver of venison are the prizes of the hunt. In lieu of venison, you can use beef heart for this recipe.

Venison heart
Equal parts dry red wine and olive oil
3 garlic cloves, pressed
½ tsp. dry oregano leaves
⅛ tsp. pepper
1 tsp. liquid smoke

Slice the heart into ½-inch slices, and marinate several hours. Cook on a hot grill. Do not cook till well-done, or heart will become tough.

Apricot Tongue

Lue grew up on a ranch in Montana, where beef tongue, heart, and liver were frequently on the dinner table, much to her dismay. Nevertheless, this recipe contains some of her favorite flavors and helps some old memories fade. The sauce is tasty on poultry and pork.

1 venison or small beef tongue

Apricot sauce:
1 package dried apricots
¾ C catsup
⅔ C brown sugar, packed
2 tsp. grated fresh ginger root
1 tbsp. soy sauce

Simmer the tongue in seasoned water or broth for 2 to 3 hours or until the meat is tender. Place water pan in place in smoke-cooker. Add some herbs if desired. Combine sauce ingredients and heat until apricots are soft. Stir frequently. Baste the cooked tongue with sauce and place on oiled cooking rack. Smoke on low for 1 hour, basting once with sauce. Or smoke in an electric smokehouse for 1 hour using 1 pan of chips. Serve remaining sauce with the tongue.

Fowl Livers

Livers from domestic and wild birds make tasty hors d'oeuvres when smoked. Smoked liver can also be used in a variety of dishes. Since liver sticks to the smoker racks even when oiled, scald it before smoking.

Scald the livers until they become firm on the outside, then remove them and sprinkle with seasoned salt. (Or season the scalding water.) Smoke 1 to 2 hours, depending on the heat in the smoker. Store leftovers in a small amount of oil in a covered jar.

Gizzards and hearts can be smoked without scalding. Since gizzards are tough, cut them into several pieces before smoking.

If you prefer, livers, gizzards, and hearts can be brined or marinated overnight before smoking. Scald livers before marinating.

Skewered Liver and Chestnuts

Liver and water chestnuts make a good combination. Thread them on little skewers and serve as hors d'oeuvres.

Place sliced water chestnuts between 2 slices of chicken, beef or venison livers that have been dipped in soy sauce. Wrap in a strip of lightly cooked bacon, skewer, and smoke about 1 hour.

Bunch of Tripe

Smoke will add flavor to mild organ meats, such as tripe.

Cook tripe in salted boiling water until tender, then pierce with a fork. Cut into strips, dip in seasoned melted butter, and cook on the barbecue grill. For a smoky flavor, add soaked chips to the hot briquettes.

Brined Smoked Liver

For this recipe, you can use beef, veal, or lamb liver sliced 1 inch thick, or whole chicken livers.

Brine:
- 4 C water
- 2 tsp. noniodized salt
- 1 tsp. sugar

Soak liver in brine for 30 minutes. Remove and pat dry with paper towels. Place in heated Little Chief smoker for 30 minutes. Brush with oil. Sprinkle with garlic or onion, salt, and pepper. Broil on the grill (oven or charcoal) for 15 minutes, turning once. Do not overcook. (Recipe from Luhr Jensen and Sons, Inc.)

Smoked Liver Pâté

This will keep in the refrigerator for a week, and also freezes well.

- 1 lb. smoked chicken livers (omit seasonings and do not cook; brine and smoke only)
- ½ lb. sliced bacon
- 1 large onion
- 4 garlic cloves
- 4 bay leaves
- 1 tsp. salt
- ¼ tsp. red pepper
- 2 tbsp. Worcestershire sauce
- ½ tsp. nutmeg
- 1 tsp. mustard
- ⅛ tsp. ground cloves

Put liver in covered pan with diced bacon. Add bay leaves, onion, garlic, salt, pepper, and Worcestershire sauce. Add just enough water to cover. Bring to a boil and cook 20 minutes. When done, discard bay leaves; add remaining ingredients and put in blender, then in molds. (Recipe from Luhr Jensen and Sons, Inc.)

Jerky

The work *jerky* is the anglicized version of the Spanish word *charqui,* which means dried beef. Many countries have different versions of jerky. *Biltong* is a South African word meaning sun-dried strips of meat; it comes from the Dutch words *bil,* buttock or rump (from which the biltong is cut), and *tong,* tongue (a reference to the shape of the meat).

Jerky is a historically important food. Early man discovered that dried meat was light enough to carry from camp to camp, and it was also easy to eat on the trail. Both jerky and pemmican, which is made in part from jerky, were staples of the Native American diet. These foods were also popular among trappers, explorers, and settlers.

Today, people consider jerky an important addition to their diet when hunting, fishing, camping, hiking, or enjoying other outdoor activities. After years of eating "trail food" (a mixture of nuts, dried fruits, candy, and coconut), hikers, campers, and others discovered what many others have known for a long time: eating jerky enabled them to sustain their energy and stamina, especially during strenuous activities. They also found that jerky tasted good and complemented the sweet flavors of dried fruits and candy.

Jerky can now be purchased at many corner markets. Unfortunately, however, most people don't know how delicious good jerky can be, since much commercial jerky tastes like spice-flavored card-board. In addition, store-bought jerky is fairly expensive.

Making jerky yourself is actually very easy and can be done at little cost. In addition, you get a much better product, and can enjoy any flavor you want. You can make it as sweet, peppery, garlicky, or as salty as you like.

In its simplest form, jerky is made of thin strips of raw meat dried outdoors, on racks. Most people prefer to do a little more than just dry the meat, however; at the very least, they season it with salt and pepper. Many go further and cure the meat strips in either a dry cure or a brine to which a variety of herbs, spices, and sweeteners have been added. The meat is then dried (outdoors, in the range oven, or in a dehydra-tor), or dried and smoked (in a commercial or homemade smokehouse, or a barbecue or smoke-cooker unit kept on low heat). To add smoke flavor, you can use either hardwoods or liquid smoke.

Traditionally, jerky in North America is made from deer, elk, moose, or buffalo, though it can also be made from birds, small game animals, fish, and domestic meats such as beef, poultry, and lamb. Bear meat was also used to make jerky by Native Americans, moun-tain men, and settlers, but today we know that it, like pork and other fatty meats, does not make good jerky, since the fat becomes rancid. In addition, these meats may contain trichinae. To avoid contracting trichinosis from pork or bear, you should first freeze the meat (see Preparing Foods for Smoking) if you want to make jerky.

Today, jerky is often not dried as much as it was in the past, nor is the meat as heavily salted. Jerky should therefore be refrigerated after smoking. If you intend to take it on trips or leave it unrefrigerated, be sure it is well dried first. If you are making jerky in hot weather, it's a good idea to add curing salts to the dry cure or brine.

Preparing the meat. The best jerky comes from good, lean cuts. You don't have to use tenderloin, but try cuts from the rump or flank, where there is less tendon. Trim away as much fat as possible, or it may turn rancid later. Because the drying process removes most of the moisture from the meat, the finished jerky will be about half the weight of the fresh meat you started with. For example, 10 pounds of raw meat will make about 5 pounds of jerky.

Generally, meat slices should be about ¼ inch thick. Slice the meat with the grain, not across it; otherwise, the jerky will crumble. Meat slices more easily if it is partially frozen.

Occasionally, when making jerky for pemmican or other uses, you may want to slice the meat across the grain. In this case, you should pulverize the jerky so that it will be easier to combine with the other ingredients.

There are three basic methods for making jerky: You can put the meat strips in a seasoned brine, you can rub the dry seasonings into the meat after soaking it in a simple brine of water, salt, and sugar, or you can omit the brining process and simply rub seasonings into the meat strips, then dry or smoke the meat.

Use crockery, glass, plastic, or stainless steel containers for brining. (Do not use any metal except stainless steel.) Mix the brine well, then submerge the meat strips by weighing them down with a plate (placed right side up so there is no air pocket), and putting something clean and heavy on top. A brick sealed in a plastic bag works well.

Stir once or twice during brining to be sure meat is evenly covered. Keep the brine and meat chilled; between 38 and 40 degrees F is ideal. Leave the meat in the brine 8 to 12 hours.

After removing the meat from the cure, rinse the meat if the recipe calls for this step. Blot the meat strips lightly with paper towels, and place them on oiled racks to dry. Place the larger, thicker strips on the bottom racks, and set the racks over newspaper. When the meat strips dry, they will acquire a glaze, or pellicle. This process will take an hour or more, depending on the temperature and humidity.

When the meat is glazed, place the racks in the preheated smoker, smokehouse, or range oven, and dry according to the recipe. The length of time needed for drying depends on the amount of jerky being made and the size of the strips, as well as such variables as temperature, humidity, and wind. Check occasionally near the end of the smoking time to see if the jerky is ready. To ensure even drying and smoking, you may need to reverse the racks about halfway through the process.

You can also make jerky out of ground meat. Brine the meat if you wish, then chill it and grind it. Add seasonings and mix thoroughly. Spread the mixture in a square-sided baking pan or a jelly roll pan lined with plastic wrap. Cover the mixture with plastic wrap, press it down to make it firm, and freeze it. The mixture should be solidly frozen, then thawed slightly for easy slicing.

If you make the mixture in a baking pan, slice it just as you would a meat loaf. If you spread it thin on a jelly roll pan, you will have strips rather than slices.

If you like, sprinkle more seasoning on each slice or strip. Place the slices or strips on racks, air-dry, then smoke.

Treat moist jerky as you would fresh meat. Drier jerky can be kept weeks or even months when refrigerated. Completely dry jerky will keep indefinitely if it is put in a closed cloth or paper bag and hung where there is good air circulation.

We encourage you to experiment with the following jerky recipes. Each brine and each smoking method will give different results. Although a given recipe may specify a particular brine, you can always use other brines. Similarly, feel free to use the drying method you prefer. If a recipe calls for an oven, you can use a smoker instead, or vice versa.

Apple Wine and Soy Sauce Jerky

Everyone has his or her favorite jerky seasoning. This is our choice for both jerky and smoked fish. It is lightly salted and slightly sweet. The result is perishable and must be refrigerated or frozen, unless it is dried completely.

  5 lbs. lean meat, sliced into strips ¼ to ½ inch thick
  2 C soy sauce
  1 C water
  1 C apple wine
  1 C brown sugar
  2 tbsp. pickling salt
  ½ tsp. onion powder
  ½ tsp. garlic powder
  ½ tsp. black pepper
  ½ tbsp. Tabasco sauce

Add more salt, if preferred, or use onion and garlic salt instead of powder.

Combine all brine ingredients in a nonmetal container, stir well, and add meat strips. Chill overnight. Remove the meat strips from the brine. Do not rinse, but blot with paper towels and place the strips on oiled smoker racks to air-dry until they acquire a glaze. (This may take several hours.)

Preheat an electric smokehouse, place the racks of meat in the smoker, and smoke using several pans full of wood chips during the process. Allow 12 to 16 hours to dry the meat.

Hunter's Jerky

If there is such a thing as a typically flavored jerky, this would be the one.

        3 lbs. venison strips
    1½ tbsp. salt
        1 tbsp. brown sugar
        1 tsp. celery salt
        1 tsp. onion powder
        1 tsp. garlic powder
        1 tsp. coarse ground black pepper
        ½ tsp. cayenne pepper
        ⅓ C soy sauce
        ⅓ C Worcestershire sauce
        ⅔ C water

Combine all brine ingredients in a nonmetal container, stir well and add meat strips. Chill overnight. Remove the meat strips from the brine. Do not rinse, but blot with paper towels and place the strips on oiled smoker racks to air-dry until they acquire a glaze. (This may take several hours.) Preheat an electric smokehouse, place the racks of meat in the smoker, and smoke using several pans full of wood chips during the process. Allow 12 to 16 hours to dry the meat.

Spicy Oven Jerky

Jerky can easily be made in the oven if you can't dry it any other way. Liquid smoke added to the seasoning mixture will give the jerky a smoky flavor.

Approximately 2 lbs. beef or venison
1 package instant meat marinade
1¾ C cold water
½ tsp. Tabasco sauce
½ tsp. liquid smoke
¼ tsp. garlic powder
¼ tsp. onion powder
¼ tsp. black pepper

Cut the meat with the grain into strips about 6 inches long by 1½ inches wide and ½ inch thick. (If you prefer drier jerky, cut strips down to ¼-inch-thick slices.)

Combine all marinade ingredients and mix thoroughly. Add meat strips and marinate overnight in the refrigerator. Remove strips and drain off excess, but do not rinse. Blot lightly with paper towels. Place strips on a rack in a jelly roll pan. Place in an oven at 150 to 175 degrees F for 3 to 3½ hours, leaving the door just slightly ajar by sticking a spatula or a long-handled spoon at the top of the oven door. Remove from the oven, cool, and store in covered container in the refrigerator.

Carne Seca

This oven-dried jerky is crisper than most jerky, and it has a great combination of flavors. If a smoke flavor is desired, add some liquid smoke.

        3 lbs. beef or venison
        2 large onions, finely chopped
        2 tsp. ground oregano, or 4 tsp. dried crushed oregano leaves
        2 to 3 garlic cloves, finely minced or mashed
        2 tsp. salt
        ½ to 1 tsp. coarsely ground black pepper
        ¾ C vinegar

Slice the meat across the grain into ⅛-inch strips. Mix all ingredients except the meat. Layer the meat and seasoning mixture alternately in the bowl, pouring the last of the mixture over the meat. Cover and chill overnight or up to 24 hours. When ready to dry, preheat oven to 200 degrees F. Shake the onion off the strips and arrange meat close together in large, flat pans such as jelly roll pans. Dry meat slowly for 6 to 7 hours, alternating the position of the pan every few hours. Leave the oven door slightly ajar so that moisture can escape. When meat has turned brown, feels hard, and is dry to the touch, remove from oven and let cool, then store in containers in the refrigerator.

Peppery Oven Jerky

Pepper is a wonderful flavor for jerky. The second time you prepare this, you may want to increase the amount of pepper.

1½ lbs. lean meat
¼ C soy sauce
½ tsp. garlic salt
1 tbsp. liquid smoke
½ tsp. pepper
1 tbsp. Worcestershire sauce

Slice meat with the grain into ⅛-inch slices. Combine marinade ingredients in a nonmetal bowl. Add meat, cover, and refrigerate overnight. Place the meat slices on an oiled rack in a jelly roll pan. Bake in an oven preheated to 150 degrees F, leaving door ajar. Turn slices every couple of hours. Allow about 6 hours to dry.

Mexican Jerky

The flavors of cumin, chili powder, and Tabasco are common in many Mexican dishes.

3 lbs. lean meat
4 tbsp. water
4 tbsp. Worcestershire sauce
2 tsp. salt
2 tsp. sugar
4 garlic cloves, crushed or pressed
½ tsp. Tabasco sauce
2 tsp. ground cumin
1 tbsp. chili powder

Slice the meat with the grain into strips ⅛ to ¼ inch thick. Combine the rest of the ingredients, and rub the mixture into the meat strips. Chill overnight in a nonmetal container. Do not rinse. Place strips on smoker racks to dry and glaze, then put in a preheated electric smokehouse. Smoke about 8 hours using 2 panfuls of chips.

Chinese Jerky

This jerky is cooked before drying, so the drying process is shortened considerably. The finished product is moister than jerky made by traditional methods.

> 3 lbs. boneless beef or venison (rump is good)
> 2 C water
> 1 tbsp. dry sherry
> ⅓ C soy sauce
> 1½ tsp. salt
> ¾ tsp. anise seed
> 5 whole allspice
> 2 tbsp. finely grated fresh ginger root
> 2 green onions, including tops
> Several small dry hot chili peppers

Combine all ingredients, except for meat, in a large pan. Bring to a boil and add the meat. Simmer, turning the meat several times, and cook until the meat is firm, about half an hour. Remove the meat from the liquid, and refrigerate until it is chilled through. Reserve the liquid. Cut the meat into thin slices across the grain. Place the slices in the reserved cooking liquid, and cook again over medium heat until the meat has absorbed the liquid, about 45 minutes.

To dry: Place the strips in a single layer on cookie sheets. For moist jerky, bake at 300 degrees F 20 to 25 minutes. If you prefer drier jerky, bake in 150- to 200-degree oven for 3 to 5 hours. Pat with paper towels to absorb any grease that may have come to the surface. Let cool. Store airtight.

Pickled Jerky

This jerky has a delightful combination of flavors.

  5 lbs. venison, beef, or other meat
  1 C orange juice (if using frozen, dilute it as you would
    for drinking)
  1 C Worcestershire sauce
  1 C soy sauce
  ¼ C brown sugar
  2 tsp. garlic powder
  ½ tsp. black pepper
  1 tsp. mustard powder
  1 tsp. onion powder
  1 tsp. mustard seed, ground or crushed
  1 tsp. celery seed, ground or crushed

Slice meat with the grain into ¼-inch slices. Combine all marinade ingredients in a nonmetal container and add the meat strips. Weigh down, cover, and let stand in a cold place overnight. The next morning, remove the strips; do not rinse, but pat lightly with paper towels. Place on oiled smoker racks until meat acquires a glaze. Smoke according to smoker directions, using several panfuls of wood chips during the first few hours.

Electric Smokehouse Jerky

This is a basic brine for jerky, and it is a good choice for those who like to add dry seasoning to the meat strips after the meat has been brined.

    5 lbs. meat, lean, well trimmed
    ½ C pickling salt
    ½ C sugar
    1 quart cold water

Slice meat with the grain about ¼ inch thick. Combine brine ingredients, add meat slices, weigh down, and refrigerate at least 12 hours. Stir once or twice to be sure all meat is evenly brined. Remove strips from brine and rinse lightly. Pat lightly with paper towels and place on smoker racks to dry for 1 hour. Have the smokehouse ready, place racks inside, and dry for 12 hours using 3 panfuls of chips during the first part of the process. (Recipe from Luhr Jensen and Sons, Inc.)

Salmon Jerky

Fish jerky is similar to smoked fish, but it is dried to a harder consistency. These are excellent flavors for salmon but are also good with other fish. Since this isn't smoked you may wish to add one tablespoon of liquid smoke.

2 lbs. skinned, boned salmon
½ C soy sauce
2 tbsp. packed brown sugar
1 tsp. grated fresh ginger root
¼ tsp. coarse ground pepper

Slice the fish into ¼-inch-thick strips (slices better if partially frozen). In a saucepan combine soy sauce, sugar, and ginger. Bring the mixture to a boil, then remove from the heat. Add the fish and stir. Let the fish stand in the marinade from 5 to 15 minutes. Remove the fish strips from the marinade and place on oiled wire racks (such as cake racks) that have been set in jelly roll pans. Sprinkle both sides of fish with coarse ground black pepper. Let air-dry for about 1 hour. Place the pans in 150-degree oven until the fish feels firm and leathery, or 5 to 6 hours. Turn the pans every hour for even drying. Cool, store airtight, and refrigerate.

Old-Fashioned Smokehouse Jerky

This recipe makes very dry jerky that should keep well.

Cut the meat, with the grain, into slices ⅛ to ¼ inch thick. Cure the meat in a brine that contains curing salts. Keep the meat and brine chilled during the brining period, which may be anywhere from overnight to 2 days. Rinse the meat and pat dry, then lightly rub a dry seasoning mixture into both sides. (This seasoning should not contain *any* salt, since the meat will have absorbed salt from the brine.) Place the strips on smoker racks, let air-dry, then smoke at a very low temperature (around 75 degrees F) for approximately 24 hours.

Sausages and Pemmican

S ausage is one of the oldest forms of processed meat. Although we don't know for sure, it was probably invented as a way to use bits and pieces of leftover meat. Since early man used almost every part of the animals he hunted, the cleaned intestines would have been a logical package for these leftovers. He must have found ways, such as cooking, drying, and smoking, to preserve the sausage mixture that was not immediately eaten.

The word *sausage* comes from the Latin *salsus,* meaning salted. The sausage of ancient Greece, the oryae, was mentioned in the *Odyssey,* so sausage is very old indeed. The earliest sausages would probably seem tasteless to us, for it was not until the Middle Ages that herbs and spices were commonly used.

Each country created its own type of sausage, based on the foods native to that particular region. Scotland used oatmeal in its sausages; cabbage found its way into the sausages of Luxembourg. The pemmican of Native Americans, a type of sausage, was made from venison and buffalo jerky, fat, and dried berries. The Italians used some of their great wines in sausage-making; the Germans, renowned for their passion for sausages, flavored theirs with beer.

The American Meat Institute divides sausages into six basic categories: fresh, uncooked and smoked, dry, cooked, cooked and smoked, and specialties.

Fresh sausages use meat that has not been cooked or cured. This group includes bratwurst, bockwurst, and weisswurst, as well as breakfast sausages in either patty or cased form. These sausages must be kept refrigerated and must be cooked before eating.

Uncooked and smoked sausages include mettewurst, Polish sausage, and smoked country-style pork sausage.

Dry sausages can be dry and hard, or semidry. Because processing involves bacterial fermentation in some sausages, they are made in a highly controlled environment. Dry sausages contain fresh, spiced meat that has been cured, then dried for long periods. Some of the salamis are air-dried for as long as six months. Other salamis are cooked, partially dried, and then refrigerated. Semidry sausages, such as summer sausages or cervelats, are partially dried in a smokehouse but are fully cooked. The texture is softer, and the sausage must be refrigerated. For home processing, some of the sausage mixtures for these types of sausages are hot-smoked or cooked in water, rather than cold-smoked.

Cooked sausages are generally made from cured or fresh meat and spices, then cooked in the casing. These include cotto salami, liver sausage, beerwurst, and blood sausage. Cooked sausages are usually eaten cold.

Cooked and smoked sausages are made of cured meat, then smoked. Mortadella, frankfurters, bologna, knockwurst, and smoked links are in this category.

Specialties include lunch meats, sandwich spreads, and other fully cooked meat products that are ready to eat and must be kept refrigerated. They may be smoked, cooked, or cured, or a combination of all three. Prepared meats such as ham, which have undergone some type of processing before distribution, are also in this category.

Making sausages can be a simple process, done at home with basic equipment. There are many advantages to making sausages at home. If you make your own, you know exactly what goes into them, and you have control over the amount of ingredients, such as salt and fat, that are added. In addition, you can use those spices and herbs you prefer. It is also less expensive to make sausage than to buy it.

When making sausages, it is helpful to break them down into two types: 1) those that must be cooked before eating, and 2) those that don't have to be cooked. Some sausages, such as garlic and chorizo sausages, can be prepared either way.

We suggest you begin by making fresh breakfast sausage patties. You can easily get started by using the following basic recipe:

For each pound of meat, add 1 teaspoon of pickling salt, ½ teaspoon of pepper, and ½ teaspoon of rubbed sage. Mix the seasonings and work them into the meat. Add enough cold water until the mixture feels somewhat sticky to the touch. Refrigerate overnight. Shape into patties and fry over low heat. Freeze any leftovers.

An easy way to begin making cased sausages is to purchase a sausage kit. See Sources for a list of suppliers.

If you are new at smoking sausages, we suggest you start with hot-smoking, since it is practically foolproof. If you don't have a regular smoker, you can make do with another type of unit. Leave cold-smoking until later, when you feel more comfortable with both sausage-making and hot-smoking.

Making dry and semidry sausages can get complicated. These sausages often require special treatment to ensure that they are safe to eat. In addition, few homes today have the proper place with ventilation and the steady cool temperatures needed for hanging sausages until they are ready to eat. These sausages should be made only by those who know the rules and have the right equipment.

We'll cover some sausages that are easy to make at home. If you wish to become an expert in sausage-making, refer to the Bibliography for suggested reading, or check your local library for sources.

Meats. The single most important ingredient in any sausage is the meat. Many sausages are made mostly from pork. Beef, lamb, and venison are also popular, and even fish can be used in sausages.

Meat can be treated in a variety of ways before it is made into sausages—it can be fresh, cooked, cured, smoked, or dried.

If you are using frozen meat, thaw it first in the refrigerator. If possible, purchase, grind, and use the meat all in the same day. Keep the meat as cold as possible, even as you are making the sausage.

Cut the meat into small chunks or cubes so that it will grind better. Cut away gristle, tendon, blood clots, bloodshot meat, and excess fat. When using venison, remove as much fat as you can, since deer fat tastes stronger and turns rancid more rapidly than other fats, even when frozen.

If you are cold-smoking pork sausage, freeze the meat first according to U.S.D.A. standards: freeze at -20 degrees F for 6 to 12 days, -10 degrees F for 10 to 20 days, or -5 degrees F for 20 to 30 days. Or you can order certified pork from most butchers. It is also a good idea to freeze game according to U.S.D.A. standards to kill any parasites.

Fat. As a home sausage maker, you can decide how much fat you want to add. A certain amount of fat is desirable in sausage mixes, since it lends moisture and flavor and helps bind the meat together. Pork fat is the best choice because of its mild flavor and high melting point. Beef fat or suet is also a good choice.

Commercial breakfast sausages contain more fat than most other sausages because they are usually fried over high heat, which toughens the meat; more fat helps keep the sausage tender. You can reduce the fat content of breakfast sausage if you cook it more slowly in a non-stick pan, add no fat to the pan, and cover it with a lid. You can also use less fat when making smoked sausages, since the low drying temperatures won't produce a tough sausage. Meat:fat ratios for sausages usually range from 3:1 to 2:1.

Spices and herbs. Besides meat and fat, most sausage recipes call for a variety of spices and herbs. Since spices give many sausages their distinctive flavor, be sure to get the best and freshest available. Store them in tightly covered containers in a cool, dark place. If you buy herbs and spices in bulk, you can store them in the freezer.

The very best flavors come from whole spices that you grind yourself. Use a coffee or spice grinder, or a mortar and pestle.

The salt used in sausage-making should be pure, noniodized salt, such as pickling or kosher salt. Salt in dry and semidry sausages is important, since it gives them their special flavor and helps destroy trichinae if the sausages contain pork or bear. Cooked and hot-smoked sausages can contain less salt; the amount used is usually determined by personal preference.

Other ingredients. Curing salts are added to sausages that are cold-smoked, and to dry and semidry sausages. Among other things, nitrite protects against botulism and trichinosis, and gives the sausage a good color. (For more details on nitrites, see Preparing Foods for Smoking.)

For a change of texture and flavor, soy protein concentrate, dry nonfat milk powder, or other products are sometimes added to sausages. Soy protein made specifically for this purpose is available from market suppliers or butcher supply shops. The soy protein sold at health food stores and some supermarkets is not as fine or flaky and therefore not as good for sausages.

Milk powder can be found at health food stores and some supermarkets, as well as some dairies. Be sure it is powder; granules don't dissolve and blend as well.

Sweeteners such as powdered dextrose are frequently listed

among the ingredients in sausage recipes. Some recipes also call for bread crumbs, which add bulk and mix in well. They can also add flavor, depending on the bread used.

Liquids may be water, milk, wine, beer, liquor, or fruit and vegetable juices, depending on the sausage. All liquids should be chilled before they are added to the sausage mixture.

Liquid smoke is sometimes added for a smoky flavor when actual smoking is either not desirable or not possible. Follow the manufacturer's directions; in general, you should allow 1 teaspoon of liquid smoke for each 5 pounds of meat. To distribute the liquid smoke more evenly, add it to other liquids before they are blended into the sausage mixture.

Grinders, stuffers, and casings. Both hand-operated and electric grinders are available in various sizes. The old-fashioned hand-operated meat grinder that clamps onto the table is suitable for small amounts of grinding if the blades are new and sharp. The grinder must have *sharp* blades, because dull blades mash meat, and mashed meat loses texture and juices. In addition, dull blades will get bogged down by the gristle and tendons wrapping around them.

If you have an old grinder, you may have to search for new blades that will fit, or get a new grinder. If you buy this type of grinder, look for a heavy-duty model with a sturdy base that clamps onto a table with a heavy screw. The grinder should have at least two blades: one for fine grinding, and one for coarse grinding.

Grinder attachments are available for some heavy-duty food mixers and some food processors. We have a heavy-duty Hobart mixer with a meat grinder attachment, which works fine if we aren't doing a lot of grinding.

If you will be doing a lot of grinding, you will probably want to invest in a small commercial grinder or take the meat to a butcher to have it ground. If you have only a small home grinder, you can get the meat ground commercially, then use your grinder to mix the ground meat with the fat and spices.

Some sausages call for a coarser or finer grind than others. Check the recipe before you begin grinding.

Stuffers are needed to get the meat from the grinder into the casings. Stuffers range from a plastic tube and dowel, to attachments for grinders or food processors, to equipment designed exclusively for stuffing. How elaborate a stuffer you get depends on how much sausage-making you intend to do.

Various do-it-yourself sausage kits are available. Some contain just the basic ingredients for the mixture; others contain basic tools such as the stuffer and casings. Still others include basic tools as well as sausage mixture ingredients.

Casings for sausages can be made from the intestines of hogs, sheep, and steers as well as from man-made materials. Sheep casings are small; beef casings are the largest. Natural, dry, salted hog casings, which need to be soaked and rinsed before they are used, are preferred by many home sausage makers who make a lot of sausages. Casings of this type are comparatively inexpensive and fairly tender. Those that are not used immediately can be resalted and refrigerated or frozen.

Some people prefer to make their own muslin casings for larger sausages. If you purchase casings, follow the directions; some commercial casings need to be soaked before using.

Making sausage. Before making any sausage, see Safety and Health. Cleanliness is extremely important when working with any food, and ground meat is particularly touchy. Start by washing your hands well and remove any rings. Make sausages during the coolest part of the day if the weather is warm, and have everything ready to go. Wash all equipment, such as the grinder and the stuffer, in hot soapy water, rinse in boiling water, then chill. Have cutting boards clean, knives sharpened, and all other equipment laid out and ready. Have the spices for each type of sausage ground, mixed, and ready.

Next, prepare the casings if they need to be rinsed and soaked. Finally, grind the meat and fat. Some recipes call for the spices to be ground in with the meat. In other recipes, the spices and other ingredients are added to the ground meat. Work efficiently so that the meat isn't out of the refrigerator any longer than necessary.

After the casings and sausage mixture are prepared, it is time to stuff the casings. Feed one end of the casing over the stuffing horn, and scrunch up the casing until it is past the horn opening. The process will differ somewhat depending on which equipment you are using, but you basically need to force the sausage mixture through the stuffing horn until the mixture appears at the horn opening.

Pull about 4 inches of casing off the horn, twist and hold the end of the casing, and force the meat into the casing. Untwist the end to eliminate any trapped air, then retwist and tie off with string. You can also use hog rings to fasten the ends of large sausages. If you are making links, push enough sausage through to fill the entire casing, then twist the casing every 3 to 6 inches to produce the links. If you see any air bubbles, prick the casing with a pin to let the air out; air pockets can cause spoilage.

Some casings come sausage-size, with one end of the casing already tied. In this case, place each casing over the end of the horn or funnel, and push the sausage mixture into the casing until it is tightly filled, then twist and tie the open end.

Drying. Most experts recommend letting fresh sausages mature by placing them on or hanging them from a refrigerator rack overnight. This method dries the outside, thereby helping to produce a better smoked product.

If the sausage contains curing salts (nitrite), some recipes suggest drying them at room temperature overnight. Other sausages containing curing salts are hung in a cold room where the temperature does not get above 40 degrees F. A fan, set on low, is placed in front of the sausages to keep the air circulating. This drying process can take weeks to three months, depending on the type of sausage. Sausages that are dried in this manner and not cooked are called matured sausages.

Smoking. Not all sausages need smoking, but most people prefer the smoky flavor.

One way to obtain a smoke flavor is to add at least 1 teaspoon of liquid smoke to each 5 pounds of meat. Prepare these sausages for baking by hanging them from the top oven rack over a drip pan, or by placing them on a rack in a large shallow pan. Bake them at 125 to 150 degrees F for approximately seven hours. Occasionally turn any sausages that were placed on a rack.

Smoking time is determined by the type of smoker used, the size of the sausage, and the ingredients.

Hot-smoking. Hot-smoking is the easiest way for beginning sausage makers to smoke sausages. Sausages to be hot-smoked do not usually need curing salts added to the mixture, since many smokers raise the temperature of the sausages to a safe level. Nevertheless, you may prefer the flavor the curing salts impart to the sausage. Always treat hot-smoked sausages as you would fresh sausages, and keep them refrigerated or frozen.

Sausages can be hot-smoked in a wide variety of units, including those designed for smoking and those designed primarily for cooking. Many homemade smokers have few, if any controls, so you must understand how they work. In some homemade smokers the sausages on the top racks may not get hot enough, so you must turn the sausages and rotate them from top to bottom. A commercial unit allows you better control of the temperature and airflow.

Regardless of the type of unit you use, you should check the internal temperature of the sausage with an instant-read thermometer to be sure it reaches at least 152 degrees F. Insert the thermometer through the end of the sausage, lengthwise, to the center. If the sausages are getting too dry too fast but the thermometer is still not registering 152 degrees F, remove the sausages from the smoker and simmer them in water for about 15 minutes, or until the instant-read thermometer registers the proper temperature.

If you aren't sure a sausage is done even after the required smoking time, don't hesitate to put it in the oven or in boiling water until the internal temperature registers 152 degrees F.

Cold-smoking. It is very difficult to cold-smoke sausages in a smoker that does not have controls for vents, drafts, and a variable heat source, since the humidity, airflow, and temperature need to be carefully monitored. Because of the danger of spoilage, careful attention must be paid to all aspects of making sausages that are cold-smoked. These sausages should have curing salts added to the mixture. (See Basic Principles.)

Sausage-making can be as simple or as advanced as you want it to be. The recipes in this chapter include a variety of sausage types.

PEMMICAN

Pemmican takes its name from the Cree Indian word *pimiyi*, meaning fat. A staple food for many Native Americans, explorers, and settlers, it traditionally consisted of a mixture of pounded dried meat, berries, and fat. Buffalo and deer were the primary sources of meat. Other meat used for pemmican included rabbit, squirrel, antelope, and beef. Sometimes nuts, wild herbs, corn, beans, and other ingredients were also added.

Today many hikers and backpackers carry jerky, nuts, and dried fruit—the very ingredients that go into making pemmican. Like their predecessors, they have found that this combination of foods gives them more energy for longer periods than does any one ingredient alone.

Since the jerky is pulverized or ground, the meat used for pemmican should not be full of connective tissues and tendons. Remove these from the meat before it is ground. The jerky must be very dry, to the point of crisp. (If necessary, dry it further in an oven.) Dry jerky can be pounded more easily and also keeps better than moist jerky.

For berries, try chokecherries, salmonberries, salal, blueberries, raspberries, or strawberries. Dry them thoroughly in the sun, then store them in tightly sealed jars, or freeze them. If you don't have dried berries, use raisins, currants, or dates.

A basic pemmican recipe consists of equal amounts of pounded-up jerky, ground dried berries, and rendered fat. Mix well. Roll into logs, make into patties, or press into small paper cups designed for candies or cupcakes.

Some pemmican recipes call for sugar. Any sweetener is optional.

Cooked Salami

This makes 25 pounds of hot-smoked salami. You may want to make a small amount at first to see if it meets with your expectations. For example, you may prefer more spices.

19 lbs. lean meat
6 lbs. pork fat
4 C cold water
½ C pickling salt
½ C white sugar
7 tsp. Modern Cure
4 tbsp. coarse ground black pepper
3 tbsp. coriander seed
3 tbsp. garlic powder
4 tsp. ground cardamom
4 tsp. ground mace

Chill the meat well. Cut into chunks, then grind through a coarse blade on the grinder. Combine all seasonings, mix well, then sprinkle over meat and mix in by hand. Grind again through a ¼-inch plate, then through a ⅛-inch plate. Stuff mixture into casings. Hot-smoke until internal temperature of sausage reaches 152 degrees F. Place in cold water to reduce temperature to 100 degrees F. Rinse briefly with hot water to remove grease, then hang the sausage for 2 or 3 hours at room temperature before refrigerating. Chill overnight before using sausage.

Italian Sweet Sausage

This a good choice for Italian dishes containing sausage. The links can be cut into chunks and added to spaghetti sauce, lasagna, or ravioli stuffing.

3½ lbs. lean pork
½ lb. veal
½ lb. lean beef
1½ lbs. pork fat
6 garlic cloves, pressed
1 C soy concentrate
2 tbsp. pickling salt
2 bay leaves, finely crumbled
2 tbsp. minced parsley
2 tbsp. dry crushed basil
1 tsp. dry crushed thyme
1 tbsp. black pepper
1 tbsp. sugar
1 tsp. nutmeg
1 tsp. crushed red pepper
2 tsp. Modern Cure
½ C rum or brandy
½ C cold water

Grind chilled meat, fat, and garlic together. Add remaining ingredients. Stuff into larger casings. Let air-dry overnight. Smoke until a thermometer stuck in sausage reads at least 152 degrees F. Dip sausages in cold water to reduce temperature to 100 degrees F, then hang at room temperature for several hours. Hang in refrigerator overnight. Makes 6 pounds.

Country Sausage

This recipe makes only 1¼ pounds of fresh sausage—just right for one or two meals.

> ½ lb. lean pork
> ½ lb. lean beef or venison
> ¼ lb. pork fat

Grind the chilled meat and fat separately. Smoke the ground meat by spreading out in a pan or fine screen and placing in a preheated smoke oven for 20 minutes using 1 pan of hardwood chips or sawdust. Chill again and mix with ground fat.

Mix together:

> 1 C bread crumbs
> Grated rind of 1 lemon
> ¼ tsp. each, sage, sweet marjoram, and thyme
> ⅛ tsp. summer savory
> ½ tsp. fresh ground black pepper
> 2 tsp. pickling salt
> Dash fresh nutmeg

Add this mixture to the ground meat and fat. Shape into patties and fry.

Coriander Sausage

Here's a recipe for all those bits and pieces of good venison meat that don't seem to fit in anywhere. Package them separately and mark "To Grind for Sausage," then freeze until you have time to make the sausage.

15	lbs. boneless venison or lean beef
6	lbs. boneless pork
⅓	C pickling salt
6	tbsp. fresh ground black pepper
1½	tsp. allspice
1½	tsp. cloves
1½	tsp. nutmeg
4	tbsp. coriander
1	tsp. garlic powder
1	tbsp. mustard seed
7	tsp. Modern Cure
2½	to 3 C cold water

Grind chilled meat and fat. Combine all dry ingredients, and mix well into meat mixture. Mix in water. Make patties, or stuff into casings. Hang cased sausages overnight at room temperature, then cold- or hot-smoke. Makes 21 pounds.

Oven Venison Sausage

If you don't want added fat in your sausage, this may be the answer.

    10 lbs. venison, ground
     4 garlic cloves, pressed
    3½ tsp. Modern Cure
     ¼ C packed brown sugar
     5 tsp. mustard seed
     3 tsp. black peppercorns
     4 garlic cloves, pressed
     4 tsp. ground black pepper
     5 tsp. liquid smoke

Crush the mustard seed and peppercorns, and add to the ground meat, along with the remaining ingredients. Mix well and refrigerate for 3 days. Divide the mixture into rolls and bake on a rack set in a shallow pan. Bake at 200 degrees F for 9 hours, turning halfway through cooking.

Garlic Sausage

This sausage is cooked after it is smoked. As the name implies, it has a good garlic flavor.

4½ lbs. lean beef or venison
3 lbs. pork butt
6 garlic cloves
4 tbsp. pickling salt
1 tbsp. coriander
2 tbsp. black pepper
¾ tbsp. mace
2¼ tsp. Modern Cure
2 C cold water

Grind chilled meat and garlic together. In a bowl, combine spices, cure, and water, then mix well with meat. Cover and refrigerate overnight. Stuff into 2 medium casings. Smoke at 90 to 110 degrees F until sausage is dry and brown. Place in hot water and simmer until instant-read thermometer stuck into sausage reads at least 152 degrees F. Makes 7½ pounds.

Chorizo Sausage

This is the spicy sausage that goes so well in many Mexican dishes. Or try it in spaghetti sauce.

- 2 lbs. venison or lean beef
- 2 lbs. pork shoulder or butt
- 2 lbs. pork fat
- 8 garlic cloves, pressed
- ¼ C wine vinegar
- 2 4-oz. cans jalapeño peppers, chopped
- ¼ C chili powder
- 1 tbsp. crushed, dried oregano
- 1 tsp. ground cumin
- 2 tbsp. paprika
- 2½ tsp. fresh ground black pepper
- 2 tbsp. pickling salt
- 1 C cold water

Chill meat and fat well, then grind once through coarse blade of grinder. Combine all remaining ingredients and mix thoroughly into meat mixture. Chill. Stuff into casings and refrigerate overnight. Smoke a few hours before cooking in water, or cook the sausages by simmering until the instant-read thermometer reads at least 152 degrees F. Makes 6 pounds.

Basic Sausage Mix

Start with this basic sausage mixture, then add the ingredients for one of the varieties below.

    5 lbs. venison or lean beef
    1 lb. pork back fat
    3 tbsp. pickling salt

Grind the chilled meat and fat together, then add salt. Add one of the seasoning mixes listed below, and knead into the meat mixture until well combined. Stuff into casings and refrigerate overnight. Hot-smoke. Makes 6 pounds. To this Basic Sausage Mix, add one of the following seasoning mixes.

Sausage seasoning:
    ¾ C dry powdered milk (do not use granules;
           mix in just enough water to make a paste)
    2 tbsp. sugar
    1 tsp. black pepper
    1 tsp. cayenne pepper
    1 tsp. ground cloves
    2 tsp. garlic powder

Combine and mix well into the basic mixture.

Pepperoni seasoning:
    ¾ C dry powdered milk (mix in enough water to make a paste)
    2 tbsp. sugar
    1 tbsp. cracked black pepper
    1 tbsp. fine ground black pepper
    3 tbsp. chili powder
    1 tsp. powdered thyme
    1 rounded tsp. crushed oregano leaf
    1 tsp. whole anise
    1 tsp. ground cumin

Combine and mix well into the basic mixture.

Salami seasoning:

   ¾ C dry powdered milk (mix in enough water to make a paste)
   2 tbsp. sugar
   1 tbsp. pepper
   1 tbsp. cayenne pepper
1½ tbsp. chili powder
   1 tbsp. garlic powder

Combine and mix well into the basic mixture.

Stuff the sausage mixture into casings. Place in refrigerator overnight to dry. Hang in a smoke oven. Hot-smoke for 8 hours. Internal temperature should read at least 152 degrees F when sausage is done. Cool, then refrigerate.

Cervelat

For this recipe, you'll need sausage seasoning mix, which is in the meat department of the supermarket or available from butcher supply houses.

   8 lbs. beef or venison
   2 lbs. pork fat
   6 garlic cloves
3½ tsp. Modern Cure
   3 tbsp. Cervelat Sausage Seasonings Mix
   2 tsp. crushed coriander seeds
   2 tbsp. black pepper
   1 tbsp. sugar
   ¼ tbsp. nutmeg
   1 C chilled dry red wine

Grind chilled meat and garlic through a small blade. Grind fat through a larger holed blade. Mix with meat. Combine remaining ingredients and mix well into meat. Stuff casings and dry at room temperature for 4 to 5 hours. Smoke at 80 to 90 degrees F for about 12 hours, then increase heat to 120 degrees and smoke another 4 to 5 hours, or until sausage feels firm. Hang the sausage in refrigerator for several weeks before eating. Makes 10 pounds.

Pemmican

1 lb. venison or beef, well trimmed, jerked to very dry
½ C raisins
4 pitted dates
2 tbsp. melted suet
2 tbsp. melted shortening
1 tbsp. lemon juice

Grind the dried meat as fine as possible, then pulverize it in a blender or with a mortar and pestle. If you have a food processor, use it. Grind the raisins and dates, then work into the meat until well mixed. Combine the suet, shortening, and lemon juice. Add to the meat mixture and blend. Work the mixture with your fingers until it holds together. Shape the mixture into small patties.

Another Pemmican

Roast about 12 large slices of jerky in the oven until they are as crisp as bacon. Put the jerky through a meat grinder, along with an equal amount of calf kidney fat. Add to the grinder fresh or frozen sour pie cherries, bing cherries, or chokecherries. If using pie cherries, add a touch of sugar or honey if desired. The fresh berries add moisture to the pemmican. Mix all together, and form into balls about the size of an egg. Melt some beef suet, and coat each "egg" with the melted fat. When the fat is solidified, wrap each "egg" in plastic wrap or aluminum foil and refrigerate.

Alaskan Pemmican

Although this recipe calls for unseasoned jerky, you can use the seasoned variety and cut down on the spices.

- 4 C powdered meat made from unseasoned, dry, brittle jerky
- 1½ C suet
- ¾ C currant jelly
- ½ C beef stock
- ½ C finely ground raisins or currants
- ½ C brown sugar
- ½ tsp. each: garlic powder, onion powder, allspice, and savory
- ½ tsp. black pepper
- 1 tsp. dried minced chives or onion

Preheat range oven to 300 degrees F. Put the jerky through a food grinder several times, then pound it until it is powdered. Melt the suet, adding the jelly as the suet simmers. Gradually add all remaining ingredients, stirring constantly. Do not add any salt unless you intend to use the pemmican immediately. Place the mixture in a baking pan, cover tightly, and bake for 3½ hours. Remove from pan and spoon into shallow pans to cool. (Individual-sized aluminum pie pans make good cooling pans.) If mixture is too thick, add a little hot beef stock. When cool, wrap in foil, and store in cool, dry place.

Meatless Fruit Pemmican

Although not a traditional pemmican, this concoction makes a great snack at home or on the trail.

- 1 C walnuts, hazelnuts, or other nuts
- 1 C raisins
- 1 C dried apricots
- 1 C dried apples
- ½ C pitted dates
- 1 C flaked coconut
- ½ C toasted sesame or sunflower seeds

Grind ingredients in a food grinder. (They may need to be put through more than once.) To this mixture, add the following:

- ½ C honey
- ½ C butter or margarine
- ½ C peanut butter
- 2 tsp. lemon juice

Mix together well and form into patties or logs. Wrap in foil and freeze until ready to use.

Other Foods

Pasta, beans, lentils, rice, and other grains, as well as seeds, nuts, cheese, bread crumbs, popcorn, and even eggs can be given a smoky flavor. Place these foods in a single layer, either in a perforated aluminum tray or on a fine mesh screen set on a rack in the smoker. The perforated tray and screening allow the smoke to better penetrate the food.

These smoked foods can add a new dimension to soups, stews, meatballs, salads, and many other dishes. Smoked nuts and seeds, cheese, and popcorn also make excellent snacks.

Smoked Nuts

Most of us enjoy snacking on almonds, cashews, filberts, and pecans. You can make your own smoked nuts at a fraction of the cost of the commercial ones.

1   C nuts
3   tbsp. oil or melted butter (optional)
½   tsp. salt (optional)

To salt nuts before smoking, soak for a few minutes in a light salt brine, or apply salt after smoking. Or use already-salted nuts. Place the nuts on a fine wire mesh or in an aluminum pan or aluminum foil poked with small holes. Smoking time depends on the kind of smoker used. For example, the small electric smokehouses take 1 hour and 1 pan of dry chips to smoke nuts. Other units call for 3 or 4 chunks of soaked wood and 2 to 3 hours of smoking time.

Smoking Seeds

Pumpkin and sunflower seeds are favorite snacks and are especially good when smoked. Smoked sesame seeds can be used in breads, casseroles, or Chinese dishes, or as a garnish. Seeds absorb smoke flavor better if they are soaked several hours, or overnight, in a salty solution. Drain well, pat with paper towels, and place on a fine screen or in a shallow aluminum pan with holes poked in it. The smoking procedure is the same as for nuts: use low heat and light smoke until seeds are dry.

Smoked Salt

With smoked salt, you can add a dash of smoke to almost any food, anytime you wish. Try it on popcorn.

Place plain table salt in a shallow aluminum pan, and set on the grill of the smoker. Smoke about 1 hour. If using a charcoal smoker, you can smoke salt while you are cooking something else. Add wet wood, if necessary; there will probably be enough heat in the coals to smoke the salt. Store in a tightly covered container.

Smoked Pasta, Beans, Lentils, and Grains

Place a fine screen over the grills of the smoker so the food won't slip through, or use an aluminum foil pan with holes poked in it. Spread the food out evenly in a single layer. When the smoker is heated, smoke the food for 30 minutes. Try different wood chips for subtle differences.

Smoked Cheese

Smoked hard cheeses such as Jack, Monterey, Muenster, Colby, Fontina, Lappi, and Jarlsberg are all good. The softer cheeses are also tasty when smoked. They absorb smoke more quickly than the hard cheeses, so you'll need to watch smoking time carefully. Too-strong smoking gives cheese an unpleasant flavor; a lighter smoke for a longer time will give better flavor to most cheeses.

Before smoking, remove any rind or wax coating on the cheese. Cut into 1-inch slices or cubes. Adjust the smoker to low or below 80 degrees F, if possible. Place pieces of cheese on heavy-duty aluminum foil or pan, or plastic hardware cloth, and smoke 1 to 2 hours. Remove before the cheese melts, unless you want it melted. While the cheese is warm, serve it on crackers or bread. For best flavor, serve at room temperature. Wrap and chill for later use.

Smoked Eggs

Hard-boil the eggs, then chill and peel them. Place the eggs on the grill and smoke 25 to 30 minutes, or until lightly browned. Eat or refrigerate immediately.

Recipes
Using
Smoked Foods

Leftover smoked meat or fish can easily be used in other dishes. Smoked salmon can go into casseroles, spreads, omelets, and sauces. The same is true for leftover sausages or smoke-cooked roast. Consider any recipe that calls for cooked meat or fish; it can be enhanced by using a smoked meat.

Consider using smoked meats and fish in any of the following:

Stew	Meatballs
Eggplant Parmesan	Spanish rice
Quiche	Hash
Casseroles	Stroganoff
Pasta dishes	Stuffed squash and peppers
Potato dishes	Cabbage rolls
Stir-fry dishes	Spaghetti sauce
Cannelloni	Kraut and ribs
Cacciatore	Appetizers
Burritos	Meat loaves
Chili	Empanadas

Smoked Salmon Spread

Almost everyone has a favorite smoked fish spread or dip. Here is another to add to your collection.

    2 3-oz. packages cream cheese, softened
 1½ tsp. dill weed
 1½ tsp. lemon juice
    ½ C smoked salmon
    1 tbsp. minced fresh parsley

Combine all ingredients, and whirl briefly in a blender or food processor until smooth. Pack into a bowl or mold lined with plastic wrap. Cover and chill. Remove from mold and garnish. Makes 1 cup.

Smoked Shrimp and Tomato Salad

This is equally good as a luncheon salad or as a side dish at dinner. It is colorful as well as delicious.

    1 lb. shrimp, smoked and chopped
    8 oz. cottage cheese
    2 hard-boiled eggs, mashed
    1 C black olives, sliced
    6 ripe tomatoes
    ¼ tsp. pepper
       Paprika

Mix the shrimp and cottage cheese together. Add the mashed eggs and mix well. Cut each tomato partway through into 6 or 8 petals to form a cup for the filling. Divide the filling mixture into 6 portions and place 1 portion in the center of each tomato. Sprinkle with paprika and place on a bed of lettuce. Serves 6.

Smoked Salmon Salad

Smoked salmon is wonderful alone or used in many other dishes, such as this main meal.

   2 C flaked smoked salmon
½ C cooked peas
¼ C minced red onion
½ C thinly sliced celery
½ C cooked green beans
½ C diced cooked potatoes
   1 head lettuce, shredded
   2 hard-boiled eggs, sliced

Dressing:
¼ C olive oil
¼ C salad oil
¼ C white wine vinegar
   2 tbsp. lemon juice
½ tsp. garlic salt
¼ tsp. Tabasco sauce
⅛ tsp. pepper

Toss salad ingredients together lightly. Mix and chill dressing. Toss with salad. Serves 6 to 8.

Sausage Casserole

This recipe came from a friend many years ago. After we started making it with our homemade sausages, we liked it even better.

     3 C cooked noodles
     1 lb. smoked, fresh pork sausage
    ⅓ C chopped onion
     1 garlic clove, minced
    ¼ tsp. salt (optional)
     1 tbsp. cornstarch
    2½ C tomato juice
     1 4½-oz. can chopped ripe olives
    ½ C grated cheddar cheese
     1 tsp. chili powder

Place sausage in a shallow pan and put it in a smoker for about 20 minutes. Cook the noodles, drain, and set aside. Fry the smoked sausage until done; drain off all but 2 tablespoons of drippings. Sauté onion and garlic in drippings. Add chili powder, salt, cornstarch, and tomato juice. Cook until the mixture comes to a boil and is thickened. Cut sausages into bite-size pieces. Add olives and sausage pieces to mixture. Mix with noodles and pour into shallow baking dish. Top with cheese. Bake in preheated 350-degree oven for 20 minutes. Serves 4.

Smoky Hamburger and Beans

This is a popular recipe. We've used it for family barbecues and picnics for many years.

Fry 4 to 6 slices bacon until crisp. Remove from pan, crumble, and set aside. Pour grease from pan, then brown 1 pound of smoked lean ground beef or venison in the same pan. Add the following:

      2 tsp. dried minced onion, or 4 tbsp. fresh onion
      2 tbsp. brown sugar
      2 tbsp. prepared mustard
      1 28-oz. can baked beans
         Bacon pieces
         Catsup to taste (approx. ¼ to ½ C)

Simmer together for 30 minutes.

Spread the ground meat in a shallow pan and smoke it for about 20 minutes. Serves 4 to 6.

Lasagna

Lasagna is one of our favorite meals. Try this one, or use your own favorite and smoke the meat first.

- 1 lb. lean ground beef or venison, smoked
- 1 small onion, finely chopped
- 2 garlic cloves, minced
- 1 28-oz. can tomatoes
- 1 12-oz. can tomato paste
- 1 tbsp. sugar
- ½ tsp. oregano leaves
- ½ tsp. thyme leaves
- ½ tsp. crushed red pepper
- 1 bay leaf
  Approx. ⅔ of 1 8-oz. package lasagna noodles
- 2 eggs
- 15 oz. ricotta cheese
- 1 lb. mozzarella cheese

About 3 hours before serving, place the ground meat in a shallow pan or on a fine mesh screen, and smoke it for about 20 minutes.

In a large heavy pan over high heat, sauté the smoked ground meat along with the onion and garlic until meat is browned, stirring frequently. Add tomatoes and liquid, tomato paste, sugar, salt, oregano, thyme, pepper, and bay leaf. Heat to boiling. Break up the tomatoes. Reduce heat to low, cover, and simmer 30 minutes. Discard bay leaf; spoon off excess fat. Prepare lasagna noodles according to package directions, drain, rinse under warm tap water, and drain again. Combine eggs and ricotta cheese. In a 9- by 13-inch baking dish, arrange half of noodles, overlapping to fit. Spoon half of egg mixture over noodles, sprinkle with half of mozzarella. Top with half of sauce. Repeat. Bake in oven preheated to 375 degrees F until heated through and bubbly, about 45 minutes. Allow more time if lasagna has been refrigerated. Serves 6 to 8.

Smoked Shrimp Frittata

A frittata is just another way to make an omelet. It is easy and makes an attractive presentation on the table. This one contains a mouth-watering combination of flavors—smoked shrimp, mushrooms, broccoli, and Parmesan cheese.

¾ C sliced fresh mushrooms
2 tbsp. butter
2 tbsp. oil
1 C smoked shrimp meat
6 eggs
½ tsp. salt
⅛ tsp. pepper
1 10-oz. package frozen, chopped broccoli, thawed and well drained
½ C grated fresh Parmesan cheese

In a saucepan, sauté mushrooms in butter. Add the shrimp. In a bowl, beat the eggs with salt and pepper. Stir in mushroom mixture, broccoli, and cheese. In a heavy skillet or omelet pan, heat the oil and pour egg mixture into pan. Cook by lightly browning the underside on the stove top, then put into a preheated 325-degree oven for 10 to 15 minutes to cook the top. Serves 3 to 4.

Smoky Potpie

Here is a recipe for a tasty potpie made from smoked venison, beef, or bird, combined with vegetables in a rich sauce and surrounded by flaky pastry. Use your own crust recipe, or try the following one, which is one of Lue's favorites.

No-Fail Pie Crust:
- 4 C flour
- 1 tbsp. sugar
- 2 tsp. salt
- 1¾ C shortening, room temperature (do not use margarine, butter, lard, or oil)
- ½ C cold water
- 1 tbsp. vinegar
- 1 large egg

Place flour, sugar, and salt in a large bowl. Cut in shortening until mealy. In a cup or small bowl, mix together water, vinegar, and egg; add to flour mixture, and stir until all ingredients are moistened. Divide dough into 5 portions; wrap in plastic wrap and chill until ready to use. (Dough freezes well.)

Filling:
- 3 tbsp. butter
- 3 tbsp. flour
- 1 tsp. salt
- ¼ tsp. pepper
- ½ tsp. crushed dry marjoram leaves
- ½ tsp. crushed dry thyme leaves
- 1 C stock—game, chicken, or beef
- ½ C cream (half-and-half)
- 2 C venison, beef, or bird, cubed, cooked, and smoked (The leftovers from a smoked roast or bird are perfect, or you could use smoked heart.)
- ¼ C chopped onion
- ½ C sliced celery
- 1 10-oz. package frozen peas and carrots (or use fresh)
- 1 large potato, cubed and cooked till almost done, drained and added to mixture

Melt butter in large pan over low heat. Stir in flour, salt, pepper, and herbs. Cook, stirring until mixture is smooth and bubbly. Remove from heat, and stir in stock and cream. Return to heat, stirring constantly, until mixture is bubbly. Cook 1 minute, then stir in meat and vegetables. Preheat oven to 425 degrees F.

Prepare the pastry. Line a 9-inch pie pan with 1 sheet of rolled-out pastry. Pour in the filling mixture and top with the remaining pastry sheet. Leave enough around the edge to tuck under the bottom pastry, then crimp edges together. Make several slits in the top for vents, and bake 35 to 40 minutes, or until filling is bubbling and pastry is golden brown. Serves 6.

Smoked Bird Stock and Soup

Bone a smoked bird, especially a big one such as a turkey, and place the bones, skin, neck, and giblets in a large pot and add enough water to cover the parts. Add several chunks of carrot, celery, and onion, along with about 6 peppercorns, 12 crushed juniper berries, and 2 bay leaves. Simmer several hours or until the remaining scraps of meat fall off the bone. Strain, and reserve the liquid. Remove the pieces of meat, package them separately, and freeze. You now have delicious stock to use for soups, gravies, sauces, and casseroles.

Taco Soup

This is one of our favorites for cold days. It is a meaty soup, with lots of flavor, and makes a great dish for lunch or supper. Serve it with hot, crusty garlic bread and a tossed salad.

>   1½ lbs. smoked ground meat
>   ¼ tsp. pepper
>   ¼ tsp. crushed oregano leaves
>   ¼ tsp. crushed basil leaves
>   1 package taco seasoning
>   6 C hot water or stock (stock gives more flavor)
>   1 8-oz. can tomato sauce
>   1 C sliced celery
>   1 C sliced carrots
>   2 large potatoes, scrubbed and diced
>   1 l-lb. can tomatoes, plus liquid
>   1 C pasta such as small spirals, shells, or macaroni
>   1 C cooked beans
>   Grated cheddar cheese
>   Taco chips

Spread the ground beef in a shallow pan or on a fine mesh screen, and smoke it for 20 minutes. Place the meat in a large kettle, and brown. Add pepper, herbs, and taco seasoning mix. Stir in hot water or stock. Cover and simmer 15 minutes. Add remaining ingredients and cook 30 minutes. If soup seems too thick, add more stock or water. Adjust seasonings to taste. Serve with grated cheddar cheese and taco chips. Serves 6 to 8.

This soup is very versatile. Feel free to substitute some of the vegetables, omit the beans or pasta, add rice, or change the seasonings.

Wild Turkey with Wild Rice

We've had this recipe a long time. In the beginning, we made it with chicken and white rice, but we found it much more flavorful when we substituted smoked birds and wild rice. This dish is good with cheese on top.

⅔ C uncooked wild rice
2 tbsp. butter or margarine
1 C chopped onion
½ C chopped celery
½ C coarsely chopped green bell pepper
1 C sliced fresh mushrooms
½ tsp. salt
¼ tsp. pepper
½ tsp. dried summer savory
½ tsp. dried marjoram
½ C blanched almonds, chopped
¼ C minced pimento
1½ C smoked turkey meat (or other smoked bird), cut up
2 C turkey stock
3 tbsp. flour

Cook the rice according to package directions, and set aside. Preheat oven to 350 degrees F. In a fry pan, melt butter and sauté vegetables. Add to the rice, along with the seasonings, herbs, almonds, and pimento. Add turkey; stir to mix.

Add the flour to 1 cup of cool stock, and mix until smooth. Heat the remaining stock in a saucepan, stirring in flour mixture. Stir and cook until bubbly and slightly thickened. Add to the rice mixture and mix. Cover and place in oven for 30 minutes, or until bubbly. Serves 4.

Recipes
for Sauces,
Butters, and
Other Seasonings

With the vast array of herbs, spices, wines, and other foods that can be used for sauces and seasonings, food just can't be boring. You can choose from an almost endless list of flavorings. Use them individually, or combine several to create pleasing condiments for different foods.

Even though the cures and marinades for smoked foods may already contain a variety of seasonings, you may still want to add a sauce. Many times marinades themselves may double as sauces for the cooked food.

SAUCES

Sauces are used to flavor and moisten other foods, and some are interchangeable as a marinade. They can also add appeal through both color and texture. For example, a velvety, cream-colored sauce over rough-textured green broccoli gives two kinds of contrasts.

The preparation of some sauces requires a number of steps, but many more are simple and easy to create. Some are very rich; others are low calorie. Some may be just a dollop that enhances a dish; others may be the basis of a dish.

Sauces that enhance smoked meats and fish vary in content and flavor. Because a smoke flavor is usually on the strong side, however, we try to select flavors that complement that flavor rather than fight it. Some of the flavors that go well with smoked foods come from herbs, yogurt, cream, cheese, fruit, and wine. Barbecue flavors are good, too.

SEASONED BUTTERS
Use seasoned butters to flavor meat and vegetable dishes, baste dry meats, or spread on French bread. Take any favorite herb or combination of herbs, garlic, onion, and chives, and mix or whip them into butter or margarine. Store the mixture in a covered container. Butters keep well for long periods in the refrigerator and are ready when you need them. Lue always has a container of herbed garlic butter on hand for meats, fish, vegetables, and French bread.

SEASONING MIXES
Keep a variety of seasoning mixes on hand. Many are available commercially, but homemade ones have more flavor, and you can use the ingredients you like.

Many seasonings call for dry orange or lemon peel. For a fresh citrus flavor, grate your own orange or lemon rind (use just the zest, the colored part of the rind). Spread the zest on waxed paper or paper towels; let it dry thoroughly, then store it in a tightly covered container. Or you can peel the zest from the fruit with a potato peeler, let it dry, then whirl it in a blender or food processor until it is grainy. The flavor of home-prepared citrus peel or zest is much more intense than the store-bought version.

Seasonings can be sprinkled on meat or fish before it is placed in the smoker. If the meat or fish has been cured first, choose a seasoning that does not contain salt, because the meat or fish will have absorbed plenty of salt in the curing process. Several of the following blended seasonings therefore contain no salt. All of the blends and salts are good on most meat, fish, game meat, and vegetables; it is mostly a matter of personal taste and what flavors you enjoy. The best thing to do is experiment.

Use the following mixes to season meat and fish, vegetables, French breads, and salads.

Dilled Yogurt Sauce

The tangy, refreshing flavors of dill and yogurt go well with most smoked fish. This sauce is low calorie.

    1 tbsp. margarine
    1 tbsp. minced onion
    2 tsp. flour
    ½ tsp. paprika
    ¼ tsp. dill weed
    ½ C skim milk
    2 tbsp. grated Parmesan cheese
    1 C plain low-fat yogurt
    1 egg, beaten
      Salt to taste

Sauté the onion in margarine until it is limp. Blend in flour, paprika, and dill. Remove pan from heat and slowly stir in the milk. Return pan to heat, cook, and stir until mixture is smooth and thickened. Stir in cheese. Blend yogurt with beaten egg and stir into sauce. Cook over low heat, stirring constantly until mixture is well blended and hot. Do not boil. Salt to taste. Makes 1½ cups.

Zesty Barbecue Sauce

This is a simple sauce that goes well with most meats, especially pork, bear, and javelina.

    1 C catsup
    ½ tsp. Tabasco sauce
    1 tsp. chili powder
    2 C water
    1 tsp. prepared mustard
    2 tbsp. packed brown sugar

Combine all ingredients. Stir to mix well. Brush generously on meat before and during smoke-cooking.

Pineapple-Ginger Sauce

Pork and poultry are enhanced by these flavors.

    1   20-oz. can pineapple tidbits
    ½ C packed brown sugar
    4   pieces candied ginger, minced
    2   tbsp. finely grated fresh ginger root

Place ingredients in a blender. Turn on and off, just enough to break down the pineapple. Place the mixture in a saucepan and simmer for 20 minutes. Brush on meat during the last hour of cooking, or brush on meat strips before smoking, or serve hot or cold alongside smoke-cooked meats. Makes about 2½ cups.

Lemon Sauce

This basic white sauce flavored with lemon and mayonnaise is especially good with poultry, game birds, or rabbit.

    2   tbsp. butter or margarine
    2   tbsp. flour
    ¼   tsp. paprika
    ½   tsp. salt
    1¼ C milk
    1   tbsp. lemon juice
    ½   C mayonnaise

Melt margarine in a saucepan. Blend in flour, paprika, and salt, stirring constantly until mixture is thickened. Cook and stir for a few minutes until flour is cooked. Stir in lemon juice and mayonnaise. Serve hot. Makes 1¾ cups.

Red Wine and Currant Sauce

Serve hot with smoke-cooked venison, birds with dark meat, or small game.

    1 tbsp. butter or margarine
    ⅓ C currant jelly
      Juice of ½ lemon
      Dash cayenne pepper
    ½ C water
    3 whole cloves
    ½ tsp. salt
    ½ C port wine

Simmer all ingredients, except for wine, for 5 minutes. Remove the cloves; add wine. Makes about 1 cup.

Citrus Mayonnaise

Serve with cold, smoked salmon, steelhead, or other fish.

    1 large egg
    ½ tsp. grated fresh lime peel
    2½ tbsp. fresh lime juice
    ¼ tsp. salt
    ¼ tsp. sugar
    2 tsp. Dijon mustard
    1 C oil

Place all ingredients, except oil, in a blender or food processor. With machine running, slowly pour in oil. Process until thick and creamy. Makes about 1 cup.

Tomato Sauce

This sauce, with its Italian flavors, is very good with shellfish.

    1 garlic clove, minced or pressed
    1 tbsp. olive oil
    1 26-oz. can tomatoes
    ½ tsp. dry basil leaves, crushed
    ½ tsp. fennel seeds
    ¼ tsp. pepper
    ¼ tsp. salt

In a skillet, sauté garlic in oil. Add remaining ingredients, stir, and bring to a boil. Reduce heat and simmer uncovered 15 minutes. Stir occasionally. Makes about 3 cups.

Almond Butter

Fish tastes wonderful with this almond butter.

    ½ C butter or margarine, softened
    ¼ C finely ground blanched almonds

Blend, cover, and chill.

Garlic Butter

This is a versatile butter—it's good with everything except desserts.

    ½ C butter or margarine, softened
    2 garlic cloves, finely minced or pressed

Blend, cover, and chill.

Horseradish Butter

Horseradish butter is excellent with domestic red meats and big game meats.

½ C butter or margarine, softened
2 tbsp. prepared horseradish

Blend, cover, and chill.

French Herb Blend

This seasoning is good with birds, venison, and small game.

½ C dry tarragon leaves
½ C dry chervil leaves
2 tbsp. dry sage leaves
½ C dry rosemary leaves
5 tbsp. dry chopped chives
2 tbsp. dry grated orange peel or zest
2 tbsp. ground celery seed, crushed

Combine all ingredients, blend well, pack into a jar, and cover with a tightly fitting lid. Store in a cool, dark place. Rub between fingers when adding to food. Makes about 2 cups.

All-Purpose Spice Blend

Use on any meat or fish.

> 5 tsp. onion powder
> 2½ tsp. garlic powder
> 2½ tsp. mustard powder
> 2½ tsp. paprika
> ½ tsp. pepper
> ¼ tsp. celery seeds, crushed
> 1¼ tsp. dry crushed thyme leaves

Combine and blend well. Store in an airtight container. Makes ⅓ cup.

Herbed Seasoning

For birds and white-fleshed fish, try this seasoning.

> 2 tbsp. dried basil leaves, crushed
> 1 tsp. dried oregano leaves, crushed
> 1 tsp. celery seed
> 2 tbsp. onion powder
> ¼ tsp. grated dried lemon peel
> ⅛ tsp. coarse ground black pepper

Combine and blend well. Store in an airtight container. Makes ⅓ cup.

Curry Blend

Use on meat, fish, or vegetables. Adjust the amount of curry powder to your personal taste.

2 tbsp. dried savory leaves, crushed
1 tbsp. mustard powder
1¾ tsp. curry powder
1¼ tsp. pepper
1¼ tsp. ground cumin
2½ tsp. onion powder
½ tsp. garlic powder

Combine and blend. Store in an airtight container. Test on a small amount of smoked meat; a strong curry flavor can fight a smoke flavor. Makes ⅓ cup.

Herbed Salt

Use on any food when you want an Italian flavor of basil and oregano.

1 C salt
1 tbsp. paprika
1 tbsp. dried basil leaves
1 tbsp. dried oregano leaves
1 tsp. celery flakes
¼ C parsley flakes

Place in blender. On low speed, add all ingredients except for salt. When blended, add the salt a little at a time. Store in tightly covered jar. Makes 1 cup.

Seasoned Salt

Use on meat, fish, vegetables, and tossed salads.

- ½ C salt
- 1¼ tsp. paprika
- 1 tsp. mustard powder
- ½ tsp. powdered thyme
- ¼ tsp. powdered oregano
- ½ tsp. garlic salt
- ½ tsp. celery salt
- ½ tsp. powdered marjoram
- ½ tsp. curry powder
- ¼ tsp. onion powder
- ⅛ tsp. dry dill weed

Place all ingredients in a blender and process until blended. Store in an airtight container. Makes about ⅔ cup.

Seasoned Salt for Beef and Venison

- 1 tbsp. salt
- 1 tbsp. paprika
- 2 tsp. garlic salt
- 1½ tsp. coarse ground black pepper

Combine and keep in a shaker container.

Seasoned Salt for Pork and Poultry

1 tbsp. salt
3 tbsp. paprika
2 tsp. crushed celery seed
2 tsp. ground coriander
1 tsp. cayenne pepper
½ tsp. allspice

Combine and keep in a shaker container.

Poultry Seasoning

Try this seasoning in stuffings and with pork and most birds.

Thinly shredded outer rind of 2 lemons
½ C parsley flakes
1 tbsp. salt
1 tbsp. dried crushed thyme leaves
1 tbsp. dried crushed marjoram leaves
1 tsp. fresh ground pepper

Dry the lemon rind, then combine with remaining ingredients. Store in tightly covered jar. Makes ¾ cup.

Parmesan Seasoning

Especially good with fish.

    ¾ C dry grated Parmesan cheese
    ¼ C dry minced parsley
    1 tsp. garlic powder
    ½ tsp. fresh ground pepper
    1 tsp. dried chives
    1 tsp. dry bell pepper flakes
    1 tsp. dried basil leaves, crushed
    ½ tsp. salt

Combine and blend. Store in tightly covered jar. Makes 1 cup.

Mild Curry Seasoning

Use for birds and fish.

    ½ C plus 1 tbsp. coriander powder
    ¼ C plus 2 tbsp. turmeric powder
    2 tbsp. salt
    1½ tbsp. fenugreek, crushed
    1 tbsp. cumin
    1 tbsp. cardamom
    1 tbsp. mustard powder
    1½ tsp. garlic powder
    1½ tsp. dill seed, crushed
    1½ tsp. cayenne pepper
    ¾ tsp. each cinnamon, ginger, mace, cloves,
        and fennel (crushed)

Combine and blend. For a hotter seasoning, add crushed red pepper. Start with ¼ teaspoon, and add according to taste. Makes about 2 cups.

Cajun Spice

Use for fish, fowl, beef, and venison.

　　1　tbsp. cayenne
　　1　tbsp. garlic salt
　　2　tsp. crushed dry basil leaves
　1½　tsp. crushed bay leaves
　　1　tsp. coarse ground black pepper
　　1　tsp. white pepper
　　1　tsp. rubbed sage leaf
　　1　tsp. ground thyme
　　½　tsp. ground allspice

Place all ingredients in a blender and process until bay leaves are finely ground. Store in an airtight container. Makes 5 tablespoons.

✦

Menus

✦

When serving smoked foods, keep in mind that a little smoked flavor goes a long way. Usually one smoked food at a meal is enough; at the most, serve two. A smoked appetizer, such as cheese, nuts, or shellfish, and a main course of smoked meat are plenty of smoked flavor for one meal.

A large buffet could include a wider variety of smoked foods. Serve a number of other foods so that guests can better appreciate the smoked ones.

With any meal in which smoked food is the entree, the other foods should complement the smoky flavor. Citrus, tangy, herbed, and mild and creamy are some flavors and textures that go well with smoked meats. For example, some chutneys and cranberry sauces are excellent complements, as are creamy and fruity molded salads. Many wines are ideal for smoked foods. Some are especially nice with smoked fish or cheese; others complement smoked red meat nicely. Follow with any dessert that is creamy, tart, tangy, or icy.

When planning a menu, think in terms of contrasting textures, flavors, and colors, such as soft versus crisp, spicy versus bland, and bright versus subdued colors.

Here are some ideas to get you started.

MENU I

Smoked turkey

Dressing of wild rice, herbs, and nuts

Spicy cranberry chutney

Whipped potatoes, with gravy from smoked turkey drippings

Green beans with mushrooms, tomatoes, oregano, and basil

Light, fluffy almond-flavored cream pie

MENU II

Spicy marinated smoked roast

Oven-fried potatoes with herb seasoning

Steamed medley of carrots, zucchini, broccoli, and onions, seasoned with garlic butter

Molded salad of gelatin, whipped cream, pineapple, and nuts

Cranberry ice or fruit sherbet

MENU III

Smoked leg of lamb with rosemary and garlic

Rice pilaf with chopped nuts and raisins

Vegetable kabobs

Ripe tomato slices marinated in olive oil, garlic, and herbs

Smoked cheese with assorted crackers and fruit

MENU IV

Smoked sausage and mushroom quiche

Grapefruit and avocado salad

Croissants or muffins and assorted jams

MENU V

Smoke-cooked ribs

Potato salad

Fresh vegetables, steamed, chilled, and marinated in Italian
dressing

Corn on the cob

Garlic-and-herb French bread

Chocolate cake

MENU VI

Smoked ham slices with pineapple

Boiled new red potatoes with parsley butter

Spinach salad with bacon, vinegar, and herb dressing

Corn muffins

Banana cream pie

MENU VII

Smoked nuts
Smoked salmon
Brown rice with chopped dried fruit and herbs
Grated carrot and pineapple salad
Sliced cucumbers in sour cream
Brandied bananas

MENU VIII

Baked beans with smoked ground meat and bacon
Pasta salad
Marinated fresh raw vegetables
Lime jello, sour cream, and pineapple mold
French bread with cheese-and-garlic spread, grilled
Lemon pie

MENU IX

Smoked sausage and noodle casserole
Artichokes with garlic butter
Fresh fruit salad with yogurt dressing
Corn bread
Raspberry ice

MENU X

Smoked whole salmon, with several sauces

Stuffed baked potatoes

Stir-fry vegetable medley

Brandied fruit salad

Angel food cake with sauce

Preserving Foods

Foods have been preserved in some manner since ancient times. Drying and curing with salt are among the oldest methods. Pickling foods is a fairly old process, too; mixtures of wine or vinegar, salt, and sometimes herbs have long been used to help preserve foods. Canning is a comparatively modern method of preservation, and the use of a canner pressure cooker is even more recent.

It is important to emphasize once again that smoking is *not* a preservative method. Smoking *aids* in preservation, but it is primarily a flavoring process. Just because a food is smoked doesn't mean it will keep without being further processed. There are some cured and smoked foods, such as very dry jerky or dry sausages, that will keep almost indefinitely without any further preservation. Most smoked foods, however, are highly perishable and must be either refrigerated and consumed within a short period of time, or frozen or canned.

Today, the most common methods for preserving smoked or smoke-cooked foods are refrigeration, freezing, canning, and drying.

REFRIGERATION
Refrigeration preserves food for only a short period. How long smoked foods will keep in the refrigerator depends on many factors, including

the type of food, how dry it is, and whether it has been cured or not. Jerky that is not completely dry will keep well several weeks in the refrigerator, but it should be frozen if kept longer. Some smoked fish will also keep several weeks in the refrigerator, though most smoke-cooked fish should be refrigerated and consumed within a day or so, or preserved by a long-term method.

Other smoked foods, such as ground meats and shellfish, usually have a short refrigerator shelf life and should be used within a day or two of smoking. A large cut of meat, such as a smoke-cooked roast or turkey, will keep well for several days longer. To preserve any fresh smoked foods for longer periods, you must use another method.

FREEZING

Freezing is easy. It takes little time to package food, label it, and freeze it. There are some drawbacks to freezing, however. For example, some frozen foods lose their texture and flavor; the smoky flavor of other smoked meats and fish may intensify when frozen. Furthermore, freezing does not kill bacteria; it merely brings the growth to a stand-still, and when the meat or fish is thawed, the bacteria take up where they left off. (This is why meat and fish should be thawed in a refrigerator.) Another disadvantage to freezing is that the freezer can shut off unexpectedly due to a power outage. Finally, frozen foods have a limited shelf life.

Many smoked meats and fish can be frozen up to a year, though fish will likely turn rancid in less time. Smoked meats and fish don't keep as well in the freezer as fresh because they tend to lose quality sooner.

Smoked foods are packaged like any other food to be frozen. The wrapping for all frozen foods should be airtight and moisture-proof. The better the packaging job, the longer frozen food will maintain its quality.

First, wrap the food tightly in plastic wrap, excluding as much air as possible. Plastic wrap helps keep air out, holds the smoked meat or fish together, and keeps moisture in.

Then wrap in one, or preferably two, thicknesses of freezer paper. Freezer paper is heavy wrapping paper that is waxed on one side. (The waxed side is a sealant, so goes on the inside.) Freezer paper also helps exclude air, and protects the inner plastic wrap. Bring the two long sides of the freezer paper up, with the edges together, and give them a double fold so the paper folds down snugly over the food. Fold each end to a point, then fold the points over twice and bring them up over the edge of the long middle fold. Use freezer tape to tape across each end and down the middle. Freezer tape may look like masking tape but is specially designed for use in extreme cold.

Heavy-duty aluminum foil can be used instead of freezer paper. You can also use heavy plastic freezer storage bags. Canning jars are good choices, depending on the food. Plastic containers with lids that seal well are popular.

Be sure to label each package or container with the contents and the date. Don't rely on your memory; otherwise you may open a package or container that holds smoked salmon when you thought it was smoke-cooked venison slices.

One excellent way to freeze smoked foods is by a vacuum packaging system, which draws most of the air out. We became acquainted with this system years ago, while on an ocean fishing trip. We caught a lot of bottom fish, which we wanted to fillet and take home, but we weren't going home for several days. A friend suggested we visit a packaging plant located near the wharf. The plant filleted, packaged, and froze the fish for us using the vacuum packaging system. Over the next few months, as we enjoyed the fish, we became increasingly impressed with the length of time it could remain frozen and still not turn rancid.

Although vacuum packaging used to be available only commercially, now there are several vacuum packing systems on the market for home use. Look for them in the larger stores that carry kitchen equipment, in sporting goods stores, or at the major sportsmen's expositions. These small units act on the same principle as the large commercial ones, by removing most of the air and then heat-sealing the heavy plastic so that the package stays airtight. Removal of the air helps prevent both freezer burn and rancidity. We have found that vacuum packaging greatly lengthens the life of all frozen meat and fish, as well as other foods.

Each brand of vacuum packager works a little differently. Our unit includes a machine that draws the air out of the packaging, then seals it. The plastic packaging material that comes with the unit is on a roll of two thicknesses of plastic sealed together along the edges.

To operate this type of unit, cut a length of plastic packaging off the roll to fit the size of the food being packaged. Heat-seal one end of the plastic in the machine. Put the food into the plastic bag and insert the open end of the bag into the machine to engage the vacuum action. The machine then draws the air from the package. As soon as the air is removed, press another lever to heat-seal the open end. (If the bag is not sealed correctly the first time, it is easy to repeat the process.) The packaged food is now ready to freeze.

After freezing, if a package does not have a tight enough seal, ice crystals will form inside the package. Use this package first.

Whichever way you choose to wrap your smoked food, freeze it as quickly as possible. If you have a lot of food to freeze at one time and you overload your home freezer, it will take too long to freeze the food; spoilage can occur during the freezing process. Instead, go to a local frozen-food locker that has a quick-freezing room (where the temperature is kept well below 0 degrees F) and have them quick-freeze it for you, then transfer the packages to the home freezer.

Smoked meat and fish can be thawed in the packaging. After thawing, however, loosen the wrapping and let some air flow around the food to keep it from getting soggy.

Some people think that freezing and thawing affect the quality of frozen smoked food, such as fish and jerky. We have thawed smoked fish slowly in the refrigerator and then warmed it slightly before eating, and we have also thawed it quickly in the microwave, being careful not to cook it. We've found the results satisfactory either way.

DRY STORAGE
Dry storage is for foods from which most moisture has been removed, such as completely dry jerky, dried fish, pemmican, and certain cold-smoked sausages. These foods are often stored in cloth or paper sacks that allow air to circulate around them, then hung in a cool, dry location.

Other foods that have been dried, such as fruits, vegetables, and nuts, can be left in dry storage. As it happens, these dried foods can often be served with smoked meat and fish. A tray of dried fruits, nuts, and smoked fish or jerky makes a wonderful snack for guests, as well as a lovely gift.

Many foods can be dried in the oven, in a dehydrator, or outside in open air. The practicality of drying foods outdoors depends on the weather. If you try to dry food in an area of high humidity, it may spoil before it dries. Choose a dry day. Put the food on screens set up off the ground and cover it lightly with cheesecloth to keep insects away. Bring the food in at night, then put it out again the next day when the air is dry.

One summer when drying apricots out-of-doors, we noticed that the fruit was slowly disappearing. We finally spotted a golden-mantled ground squirrel stealthily hauling away dried apricots to his winter cache. Apparently, the cheesecloth we had spread over the fruit to keep the flies off had not deterred him at all.

Jerky, dried fruits, vegetables, and nuts keep well for long periods. Jars with tight-fitting lids make good storage containers; not only do they keep out insects and dust, they also make it easy to see the contents. For large amounts of dried foods, consider the gallon-size glass or plastic jars with screw lids. Sometimes these are available at low cost from restaurants that buy catsup, mustard, salad dressings, and mayonnaise by the gallon. Label your containers. You might be able to see the contents inside a glass jar, but by recording dates you can use up the oldest food first.

Remember, the food *must* be thoroughly dry before storing, since any moisture will lead to spoilage.

CANNING

Before the advent of freezers, canning was the primary means of preserving foods of all kinds. Although canning is a long, involved process, many people still choose this method of preservation for a variety of reasons:

- Canned foods can be stored in quantity and are easy to keep.
- Canned foods make excellent gifts and are economical to store, since there is no maintenance cost.
- Proper canning prevents spoilage by killing bacteria and mold.
- Canning tenderizes meats.
- Some foods taste better when canned.

If you intend to can food, set aside a large block of time. Once the process has been started, you will need to continue without interruptions. Take your time, and be sure to follow directions for whatever you are canning, down to the last detail. Improperly canned meat, fish, or other foods can lead to botulism, which is a deadly poison (see Safety and Health).

When smoking meats and fish to be canned, go a little bit lighter on the smoking process, since canning tends to intensify the smoke flavor.

Smoked meats and fish are canned by the same process as unsmoked raw meat and fish. Food must be thawed, not frozen, and cleanliness is of the utmost importance.

A canner pressure cooker is an absolute necessity if you are canning meat, fish, or other low-acid foods. Be sure it is a canner pressure cooker. Follow the manufacturer's detailed directions carefully, especially the instructions for checking pressure gauges. If your pressure canner uses a dial pressure gauge, check it for accuracy at least once a year. If the pressure is off by more than one pound, replace the gauge. (Your county extension office can tell you where to have the testing done.) Every canning season, before you begin the process, check the gasket on the pressure canner lid and replace it if necessary. Few things are more frustrating than having a large quantity of food ready to can, only to discover the gasket on the lid of your pressure canner has given out.

The pressure canner is the only way to heat the food to 240 degrees F, the temperature required to kill the botulism spores and bacteria that contaminate food. A temperature of 170 degrees F will stop yeast and mold spores from growing, but 240 degrees F is absolutely necessary for meats, fish, and low-acid foods, such as vegetables.

Any canned food should be thrown away immediately if it shows signs of spoilage, such as bulging lids or can ends, leakage, spurting liquid, mold, or an off-odor. Do *not* taste it, and remember that spoiled food does not necessarily have a bad odor. Put any food you think is spoiled down a garbage disposal, or boil it for 30 minutes to detoxify it, then cool and discard it. Thoroughly clean any equipment that has come into contact with the contaminated food. Wash your hands if you have touched the food.

In addition to the pressure canner, you will need jars and lids, or cans and a sealer, depending on your choice. You will also need a timer to time the processing, a jar lifter or tongs for lifting hot containers out of the pressure canner, some mitts or pot holders to protect your hands, and hot pads or wooden cutting boards to set hot jars or cans on.

Use glass jars designed for canning. Do not use old jars such as mayonnaise jars, because the glass is not made for canning. Also, canning rings do not always screw on these jars correctly.

Canning jars come in half-pints, pints, and quarts. Check each jar for cracks and chips. Rings and lids are the most commonly used for sealing. The lids have a self-sealing compound on the underside. When properly processed, the lid seals so well that after the jar is completely cool, the rings can be unscrewed and removed. Some lids have a dome in the center that indents during the canning process when they are sealed. The wide-mouth style of jar is best for canning smoked meats and fish, since it allows easy access for getting the pieces in and out of the jars.

The basic process for canning, using jars, is as follows: Wash all utensils and containers in hot, soapy water, and rinse well in boiling water. (The jars themselves will be sterilized during the processing.)

Thaw all frozen meat and fish before canning. Cut the food into appropriate sizes for the containers. Pint- and half-pint jars are a good choice for smoked meats and fish, since only a small amount of these foods is usually eaten at one time. Pack the meat or fish into the jars, leaving a 1-inch head space. Food can be packed loosely or tightly.

Add boiling liquid. This liquid is usually a meat broth, but in the case of fish, you can add several tablespoons of an oil instead of water or broth. The choice of liquid depends on the food you are canning. A broth from which fat has been skimmed is ideal for low-fat diets, and gives much more flavor than water.

Wipe the mouth of each jar, set a hot lid on top, and add the ring, screwing it on tight. Pour approximately 4 quarts of water into the pressure canner, but do not heat until you are ready to begin processing. Put the jars in the canner. (A double layer of pint jars can be processed in most pressure canners at one time, with a rack between the layers.) Put the lid of the pressure cooker in place and lock it.

Be sure to vent air from the pressure cooker for at least 10 minutes before closing the steam vent. Venting prevents the development of cold spots, which can cause food to be underprocessed.

Place the pressure regulator on the petcock, and heat the canner until the pressure reaches 10 pounds. Start counting the processing time at this point. Keep the pressure constant. Processing time is determined by the kind of food. Follow the manufacturer's directions, since the design of each pressure cooker is slightly different. For example, there are weighted gauge canners and dial gauge canners, and the required pounds of pressure vary slightly with each. When the time is up, remove the canner from the heat, and set aside to cool. Do not touch it until it is cool.

Test the seals on all jars within 24 hours. If a jar didn't seal properly, use a new lid, and reprocess the jar in the canner for the entire length of time. Or refrigerate the food from that jar and use it as soon as possible. When canning at high altitudes, you will need to adjust the pressure requirements. Follow the directions that came with your pressure canner or the information in a reliable canning book.

If you use cans instead of jars, check to be sure they have no dents or holes. Follow the directions that come with the cans, or get detailed information from the other reliable sources on canning. You will also need a sealer for canning in cans. Unlike canning jars, cans are not reusable.

There are slight differences in the procedures for canning red meats, poultry, fish, and shellfish. For example, smoked fish is canned immediately after smoking and cooling. To keep smoked seafood moist, you will usually need to add about 2 tablespoons of oil to each pint jar. Pint-size or even half-pint containers are good for smoked fish, since a little of this food goes a long way. As a general rule, you should allow up to ⅔ of a pound of smoked fish per pint. Don't worry about removing the small bones in fish before canning; these are softened during the process and become edible.

We suggest you get detailed canning instructions for the type of meat or fish you wish to process. Step-by-step information on canning specific foods, including smoked foods, is available from county extension services, the U.S. Department of Agriculture, and from some state fish and game departments, as well as from a wide variety of cookbooks. A small canning cookbook is often included with a canner pressure cooker, and canning recipe books are put out by the makers of canning jars.

Tables

APPROXIMATE BRINING TIMES

The amount of time for brining meats and fish is highly variable. If the meat or fish is being cured (a curing agent is added to the brine), it takes longer than if the food is simply brined. Brining time also depends on the thickness of the meat or fish. For example, a ½-pound thick chunk will take longer to cure than a thin piece that weighs the same. If the meat or fish is being marinated, the length of brining time depends on how much flavor you want the food to absorb, or how tender you want the meat.

Meat or fish that is being cured, brined, or marinated should be kept chilled. Any meat or fish that is in a brine should be stirred once a day, since the heavier ingredients sink to the bottom.

Meats

	Weight in Pounds	Time
Roasts	3 to 4	up to 5 days
	5 to 10	up to 6 days
Pork roasts	3 to 8	up to 8 days
Pork chops	6 to 12	5 to 10 hours
Pork ribs	5	5 to 10 hours
Lamb leg or shoulder	5 to 7	up to 8 days
Lamb chops	6 to 12	5 to 10 hours
Liver		1 to 8 hours
Jerky		8 to 12 hours

Poultry

	Weight in Pounds	Time
Split or cut-up chicken	1 to 4	4 to 10 hours
Whole chicken	2 to 3	4 to 10 hours
	5 or more	6 to 24 hours
Turkey	8 to 12	12 to 24 hours
	13 to 24	12 to 40 hours
Small birds	1 to 3	4 to 6 hours
Duck, goose, pheasant	3 to 5	4 to 10 hours

Fish

Increase time by 25 percent for oily fish and fish with skin.

	Weight in Pounds	Time
Fish	under 1	¾ to 1 hour
	1 to 2	2 to 4 hours
	2 to 3	3 to 4 hours
	3 to 4	4 to 5 hours
	4 to 5	5 to 6 hours
Steaks	1 inch	6 to 8 hours
	2 to 3 inches	24 hours
Fillets		1 to 2 hours
Clams		½ hour
Oysters		⅔ hour
Shrimp, crayfish		up to 2 hours

APPROXIMATE SMOKE-COOKING TIMES

The times listed for cooking and smoking foods in a gas smoke-cooker are only approximations. It takes longer to cook food in a charcoal smoker than in a gas cooker. Times vary depending on the brand of smoke-cooker used. Some units will have a digital temperature gauge; others will read "low," "ideal," or "high." The best temperatures for smoke-cooking range between 170 and 200 degrees F, which is the "ideal" range.

When smoke-cooking meat, use a meat thermometer. Insert the thermometer into the thickest portion of the meat, but don't let it touch the bone. It is difficult to use a thermometer with fish. You can check to see if the fish is done by inserting a fork in the thickest portion and twisting; it should flake easily when done. Or look for a change from translucent to opaque; an opaque fish is done.

Fresh pork should be cooked until the internal temperature reaches 185 degrees F, and cured or smoked pork should reach 170 degrees F. Cook spareribs until the meat pulls easily from the bone.

	Weight in Pounds	Hours to Cook
Pork	per pound	¾
Pork roasts	3 to 4	2 to 4
	4 to 8	4 to 8
	8 to 10	8 to 10
Spareribs	5	3 to 5
Pork chops	full grill	3 to 4
Fresh pork sausages (1 inch thick)	per pound	¾ to 1
Fresh ham	10 to 15	8 to 12
Cooked ham	any size	3 to 5
Boneless beef roasts	3 to 5	3 to 4
	5 to 7	4 to 6
	8 to 10	7 to 8
Lamb roasts	3 to 4	3 to 4
	5 to 7	4 to 7
Lamb chops	per pound	¾

	Weight in Pounds	**Hours to Cook**
Turkey	12 to 14	6 to 8
	15 to 18	9 to 12
Turkey breast	4 to 5	3 to 5
Chicken	3 to 4	3 to 4
Chicken quarters (1 to 4 chickens)		2 to 3
Duck and pheasant	3 to 5	4 to 5
Dove, quail, squab	full grill	2 to 3
Fish fillets, steaks, and small whole fish		to 2
Whole fish	3 to 6	2½ to 5
Shrimp	full grill	¾ to 1
Lobster tails	full grill	1 to 3
Liver	2	1 to 2
Sweetbreads	2	1 to 2
Meat loaf	2	2 to 4

TEMPERATURES

Food	Fresh	Smoked or Cooked
Ham	185°	130°
Pork	185°	170°
Poultry	185°	

	Rare	Medium	Well done
Beef	140°	160°	170°
Lamb	160°	170°	180°–185°

BASIC PICKLING SOLUTION (1 GALLON)

3 pints water

2 quarts white vinegar (5 percent)

2 cups sugar (granulated)

4 tbsp. salt (pickling salt)

¾ cup spices (pickling spices)

2 small onions (white)

½ tsp. garlic (dry, chopped)

2 garlic cloves (fresh, pressed)

If a sweeter product is desired, add more sugar; do not use less vinegar.

FAT CONTENT OF COMMON FISH
All popular shellfish have a low-fat content.

Albacore, Pacific	moderate
Bass, largemouth and smallmouth	low
Bluefish	low
Bluegill	low
Bullhead	low
Butterfish	moderate
Carp	low to moderate
Catfish	low
Chub	high
Cod	very low
Crappie	low
Croaker	low
Drum, black	low
Eel	moderate to high
Flounder	low
Grouper	low
Haddock	low
Hake	low
Halibut	very low
Herring	moderate
Kingfish	very low
Lingcod	very low
Mackerel	high
Mahimahi	low
Mullet	moderate
Muskie	low
Ocean perch	very low
Perch, yellow	low
Pickerel	low
Pike	low
Pollack	low
Pompano	moderate
Porgy	low
Rockfish	very low
Sablefish	moderate to high
Salmon	high
Sea bass	very low
Sea trout	low
Shad and roe	high
Shark	low
Sheepshead	low
Smelt	low to moderate
Snapper	low
Sole	low
Spot	low
Striped bass	low
Sturgeon	high
Swordfish	moderate
Trout	moderate to high
Tuna	high
Turbot	low
Whitefish	moderate
Whiting	low

NUTRITIONAL VALUES
Calories per 3½-ounce serving

	Approximate Calories		Approximate Calories
Beaver	248	Quail	168
Duck	138	Rabbit	135
Muskrat	153	Raccoon	255
Opossum	153	Turkey	190
Pheasant	162	Venison	126

Grams of fat and cholesterol per 3½-ounce serving

	Fat	Cholesterol		Fat	Cholesterol
Antelope	.9	112	Mule deer	1.4	107
Cottontail		77	Snow goose	3.6	142
Elk	.9	67	U.S.D.A. choice beef	6.5	72
Jackrabbit		112			
Moose	.5	71			

Grams of fat and protein per 100 grams

	Fat	Protein		Fat	Protein
Beaver, roasted	13.7	29.2	Quail	6.8	25
Crayfish	.5	14.6	U.S.D.A. choice beef	25.1	17.4
Frog legs	4	21			
Opossum	10.2	30	Venison	4	21
Pork	26.7	15.7			

Grams of fat and amount of calories per pound

	Fat	Calories		Fat	Calories
Beef sirloin	95	1,175	Rabbit	18	490
Quail	27.8	686	Venison	18	572

LEAN AND FAT GAME

Antelope	Lean	Opossum	Fat
Bear	Fat	Pheasant	Lean, white meat
Beaver	Fat	Pigeon	Lean, dark meat
Buffalo	Lean	Quail	Lean, white meat
Caribou	Lean	Rabbit	Medium lean
Chukar partridge	Lean, white meat	Raccoon	Fat
Deer	Lean	Ruffed grouse	Lean, white meat
Dove	Lean, dark meat	Sharptail grouse	Lean, dark meat
Duck	Fat, dark meat	Snipe	Lean, dark meat
Elk	Lean	Squirrel	Medium lean
Goose	Fat, dark meat	Turkey, wild	Lean, white meat
Hungarian partridge	Lean, dark meat	Woodchuck	Fat
Moose	Lean	Woodcock	Lean, dark meat
Muskrat	Fat		

WOOD FLAVORS

Some of the following woods, such as hickory and mesquite, are also available in charcoal. Charcoal gives a somewhat different flavor to food than does the same wood in chip or chunk form.

Alder: Mild, sweet. Use for salmon, swordfish, pork, poultry, and game birds with light meat.

Apple: Delicate, fruity. Use for chicken, turkey, pork, and salmon. Not good with swordfish.

Cherry: Mild, fruity. Use for poultry, pork, beef, and salmon. Not good for swordfish.

Grapevine: Tart. Good for poultry, but not for lamb, swordfish, or salmon. Use for red meats, goat, antelope, and upland game birds.

Hickory: Strong and pungent, or delicate and sweet, depending on the meat or fish it is used for. We like it for red meats as well as big and small game.

Maple: Sweet, mild. Use for poultry, pork, and small game birds.

Mesquite: Strong, sweet. Use for big and small game, and game birds with dark meat. Not as good with lamb; gives swordfish a bitter taste.

Mountain mahogany: Mild. Use for poultry, beef, and salmon. This wood may be difficult to obtain.

Oak: Medium. Use on meats with stronger flavors, such as goat, antelope, and mutton.

METRIC CONVERSION

U.S. Standard measurements for cooking use ounces, pounds, pints, quarts, gallons, teaspoons, tablespoons, cups, and fractions thereof. The following tables enable those who use the metric system to easily convert the U.S. Standard measurements to metric.

Weights

U.S. Standard	Metric	U.S. Standard	Metric
.25 ounce	7.09 grams	11 ounces	312 grams
.50	14.17	12	340
.75	21.26	13	369
1	28.35	14	397
2	57	15	425
3	85	1 pound	454
4	113	2	907
5	142	2.2	1 kilogram
6	170	4.4	2
7	198	6.6	3
8	227	8.8	4
9	255	11.0	5
10	283		

Liquids

U.S. Standard	Metric	U.S. Standard	Metric
1/8 teaspoon	.61 milliliter	3/8 cup	90 milliliters
1/4	1.23	1/2	120
1/2	2.50	2/3	160
3/4	3.68	3/4	180
1	4.90	7/8	210
2	10	1	240
1 tablespoon	15	2	480
2	30	3	720
1/4 cup	60	4	960
1/3	80	5	1200

To convert	multiply	by
Ounces to milliliters	the ounces	30.
Teaspoons to milliliters	the teaspoons	5.
Tablespoons to milliliters	the tablespoons	15.
Cups to liters	the cups	.24
Pints to liters	the pints	.47
Quarts to liters	the quarts	.95
Gallons to liters	the gallons	3.8
Ounces to grams	the ounces	28.35
Pounds to kilograms	the pounds	0.45
Inches to centimeters	the inches	2.54

To convert Fahrenheit to Celsius: Subtract 32, multiply by 5, divide by 9.

Sources

EQUIPMENT AND SUPPLIES

Arkla Products Company. 1600 Jones Road, Paragould, AR 72450. 501-236-8731. *Produces Embermatic and Arkla gas grills and manufactures for Sears under the Kenmore label. Many accessories, such as grill baskets, warming racks, and rotisseries, are available. Also makes a cast iron smoke box, which makes smoking in gas grills convenient.*

The Brinkman Corporation. 4215 McEwen Road, Dallas, TX 75244. 214-387-4939. *Manufactures a variety of models of smoke-cookers, smoker grills, and cooker/fryers, as well as accessories.*

Buck Knives, Inc. P.O. Box 1267, El Cajon, CA 92022. 619-449-1100 or 800-326-2825. *Manufactures cutlery, hunting and pocket knives, and sharpening accessories.*

Charcoal Companion. 1150 6th Street, Berkeley, CA 94710. 415-525-3800 (in California) or 800-521-0505. *Product line includes many different grilling grids and accessories, such as long-handled forks, tongs, brushes, grilling baskets, and chimney starters. Also carries smoking herbs, basilwood, and hardwood chips.*

Coleman Outdoor Products, Inc. P.O. Box 2931, Wichita, KS 67201-2931. 316-261-3211. *In addition to many types of outdoor equipment for campers, Coleman makes a propane and briquette smoke-cooker.*

Colorado Aggregate Company. 8388 Sharon Road, Newburgh, IN 47630. 812-858-5104. *Produces hickory and mesquite wood-smoking chips, ceramic briquettes, lava rocks, and hickory liquid smoke.*

Consolidated Cutlery Company, Inc. 696 N.W. Sharpe Street, Port St. Lucie, FL 34983. 305-878-6139. *Makes a variety of knives.*

Cumberland General Store. Route 3, P.O. Box 81, Crossville, TN 38555. 615-484-8481 (in Tennessee) or 800-334-4640. *Carries "Home Meat Curing Guide," a 38-page booklet by Morton International, Inc. This store also carries a Morton Sugar Cure (with or without smoke flavor); Morton Tender-*

Quick (a fast cure); Morton Meat, Poultry, and Sausage Seasoning (a complete mixture to make pork sausage and meat loaf); and a meat pump.

Enviro-Pak, A Division of Tech-Mark, Inc. 15450 S.E. For-Mor Court, Clackamas, OR 97015. 503-655-7044 or 800-223-OVEN. *Carries a variety of different food processing ovens, smokers, and dryers. The smaller cabinet ovens may be of interest to the serious home smoker.*

Frost Cutlery Company. P.O. Box 21353, Chattanooga, TN 37421. 615-894-6079. *Makes cutlery items.*

Gerber Legendary Blades. 14200 S.W. 72nd Avenue, P.O. Box 23088, Portland, OR 97233. 503-639-6161. *Makes many high-quality knives.*

Griffo Grill. 1400 N. 30th, Quincy, IL 62301. 217-222-0700. *Carries a number of products, such as grill toppers, grill racks, seafood racks, smoking racks, charcoal chimneys, and olive wood briquettes.*

Harpco. 3600 Rhayer Court, Suite 110, Aurora, IL 60504. 708-978-8000. *Carries thermometers, lava rocks, mesquite and hickory chips, steel smoker trays, cookbooks, cleanup equipment, and Griffo Grills. This company is a good source for accessories and replacement parts for a variety of brands of barbecue units.*

Heller's Seasoning and Ingredients, Inc. 6363 W. 73rd, Bedford Park, IL 60638. 708-594-6630. *Makes seasonings for sausages and for curing meat and fish.*

Hickory Specialties, Inc. P.O. Box 1669, Brentwood, TN 37027. 800-251-2076. *Makes Nature-Glo briquettes, chips, and fire starter. This is the source for Jack Daniel chips and charcoal briquettes, as well as for hickory and mesquite briquettes and chips.*

Kershaw Knives, Kai Cutlery USA, Ltd. 25300 S.W. Parkway Avenue, Wilsonville, OR 07070. 503-682-1966. *Manufactures a wide assortment of fine-quality knives.*

Kitchen Secrets of Dallas. P.O. Box 151467, Dallas, TX 75315. 214-324-2434. *Makes packets of seasoning for various kinds of sausages.*

Kiwi SmokeOven. 3975 E. 56th Avenue, A4, Commerce City, CO 80022. 303-296-7900. *Manufactures a small box-style unit that fast-cooks using Sterno or denatured alcohol.*

Luhr Jensen and Sons, Inc. P.O. Box 296, Hood River, OR 97031. 503-386-3811 or 800-366-3811. *Produces the Little Chief Smokehouse and the Big Chief Smokehouse, which holds up to 50 pounds of meat. Both come in top-loading or front-loading models, as well as a space-saver model. Carries five different flavored hardwood chips and a sausage-making kit.*

Market Supply Company. 139 S.E. Taylor, Portland, OR 97214. 503-239-4990. *Carries many kinds of seasonings and cures, as well as casings and other items needed for curing meats. Check the phone book in your area for similar companies.*

McCormick & Company, Inc. 908 N. Elm, Hinsdale, IL 60521. 708-323-5000. *Makes spices and herbs.*

Meco. 1500 Industrial Road, P.O. Box 1000, Greeneville, TN 37743. 615-639-1171. *Produces water smokers, electric and charcoal barbecue grills, and accessories. Also carries hickory and mesquite chips and chunks.*

Morton International, Inc. 100 N. Riverside Plaza, Chicago, IL 60606-1597. 312-807-2000. *Carries products for curing meat.*

New Braunfels Smoker Company. P.O. Box 310096, New Braunfels, TX 78131. 512-629-6000. *Manufactures the Hondo Smoker, a large unit with an off-set firebox and dual chambers for grilling, smoking, and slow-cooking. Features a temperature gauge, a smokestack, and racks on the front. Best used with hardwood but can also be used with briquettes.*

Pop Geer, Inc. 439 W. 2nd, Eugene, OR 97401. 503-484-9171. *Manufactures several sizes of the Totem Food Smoker, which is an electric smoke oven.*

Pyramid, Inc. Outdoor Cooking Systems, 3292 S. Highway 97, Redmond, OR 97756. 800-824-4288. *Manufactures the Pyramid Portable Barbecue-Stoves.*

T.S. Ragsdale Company, Inc. P.O. Box 937, Lake City, SC 29560. 803-394-8567. *Makes Embers Charcoal Briquettes, hickory and mesquite chips, and other charcoal products. A division of the Ragsdale Company.*

Red Arrow Products Company, Inc. P.O. Box 1537, Manitowoc, WI 54221-1537. 414-683-5500. *Produces natural liquid and dry smoke flavorings and related equipment for food industries.*

The Sausage Maker. 26 Military Road, Buffalo, NY 14207. 716-876-5521. *Upon request the company will send a free catalog, which contains a full line of sausage-making supplies and small equipment, such as grinders and stuffers.*

Schrade Cutlery. Route 209 N., Ellenville, NY 12428. *Makes primarily pocket and hunting knives.*

Sikes Enterprises. P.O. Box 1208, 1437 Esplanade Avenue, Klamath Falls, OR 97601. 503-882-3336. *Makes seasoned brine mix for jerky, brine mix with garlic, and a seasoned brine mix for fish. Also makes a jerky cure with a smoke flavor for those without a smoker.*

Spice 'n Slice. P.O. Box 26051, Phoenix, AZ 85068-6051. 602-861-4094. *Makes packets of seasonings to add to ground meat to make jerky, salami, pepperoni, and other sausages.*

Sunbeam Leisure Products Company. 4101 Howard Bush Drive, Neosho, MO 64850-9164. 417-451-4550. *Largest maker of gas grills and third largest maker of charcoal grills in the United States. Makes a wide variety of grills, from the popular portable tabletop styles to the large deluxe wagon- or cart-style grill. Some grills can operate on natural gas. One type of grill has four independently controlled burners.*

Weber-Stephen Products Company. 200 E. Daniels Road, Palatine, IL 60067-6266. 708-934-5700. *Manufactures charcoal kettles and smokers, many models of gas barbecues, barbecue tools, FireSpice cooking chunks, chips, and bits. Also carries fire starters, charcoal, and gas accessories. Products of special interest are Smokey Mountain Cooker, Flamgo, FireSpice Woods, and Steam-N-Chip Smoker for gas grills.*

INFORMATION
National Fisheries Institute. 111 E. Wacker Drive, Chicago, IL 60601.

Northeast Fisheries Center. Gloucester Laboratory, Emerson Avenue, Gloucester, MA 01930.

Ohio Department of Natural Resources. Fountain Square, Columbus, OH 43224. *Publishes "Fish Smoking," Publication No. 64.*

Oregon State University Extension Service. Ballard Hall, Room 102, Oregon State University, Corvallis, OR 97331-3606. 503-733-2711. *Carries bulletins on smoking, pickling, and canning seafoods, as well as information on venison and other game foods.*

Publications Office, Department of Agriculture. Washington, D.C. 20250, or Government Printing Office, Washington, D.C. 20402. *Carries pamphlets on food and health safety. Information on meats, fish, and smoking is found in Home Bulletins and Farm Bulletins. Write to the Meat Inspection Division for information on sausage-making and freezing pork to destroy trichinae.*

U.S. Department of Health, Education and Welfare, Public Health Services, Food and Drug Administration. 5600 Fishers Lane, Rockville, MD 20852. *Carries information on the home-drying of meats in the Code of Federal Regulations.*

University of Alaska's Marine Advisory Program. 2221 E. Northern Lights Boulevard, Suite 220, Anchorage, AK 99508. *Will provide detailed information on the care of freshly caught fish.*

University of California, Sea Grant Marine Advisory Program. 554 Hutchinson Hall, Davis, CA 95616. *Carries "Smoked Shark and Shark Jerky for Home and Trail," by J. Richard and R. Price (Marine Brief #14); "Smoking Fish at Home," by M. Tate, et al.; and "Spiced and Pickled Seafoods," by R. Price (Marine Brief #6).*

Glossary of Terms

Acidic foods. Foods such as lemons, oranges, pineapple, wine, and some tomatoes. Foods that normally contain from 0.36 to 2.35 or more percent natural acid.

Age. To hang meat, usually in a chilled area, in order to tenderize it.

Ascorbic acid. Vitamin C. Often used when canning fruits, to help keep the color fresh. It is sometimes used in sausage recipes to help retain the red color of meat.

Bacteria. One-celled microorganisms that can only be seen under a microscope. Some bacteria cause diseases; others are needed for fermentation, nitrogen fixation, and other processes.

Barbecuing. Commonly defined as hot, fast cooking over an open grill. Usage of the term varies in different areas of the country.

Bard. To lay slices of fat over meat while it is cooking, to prevent the meat from drying out.

Baste. To spoon or brush an oily or liquid mixture over food for the purpose of preserving moisture and adding flavor.

Botulism. A deadly form of food poisoning, usually caused by improper home canning of meats, fish, and vegetables or other low-acid foods. It is tasteless and odorless.

Braise. To brown food, usually meat, in a small amount of fat, then cook it in a small amount of water in a covered pan.

Brine. A mixture for curing meats and consisting of salt, sugar, spices, and sometimes other ingredients, to which a liquid is added.

Canner pressure cooker. A large kettle designed with gauges and a seal-tight lid, and used to cook foods at temperatures higher than the boiling point. It is essential equipment for canning meat, fish, and other low-acid foods.

Casings. Tubes of fabric, fiber, or cattle or sheep intestines in which a sausage mixture is stuffed.

Certified pork. Pork meat or pork products that have been frozen to destroy trichinae, which can cause the disease trichinosis.

Charcoal. A black form of carbon produced by burning or oxidizing wood or other organic material in large kilns, from which air is excluded.

Charcoal briquettes. Charcoal plus a binding agent, compressed into small shapes to use as fuel.

Cold-smoking. The process of drying and smoking foods at very low temperatures for days or weeks. Cold-smoking is used on foods such as hams, bacon, some sausages, and some smoked fish.

Complete cure. A dry mixture of salt, curing salts, and spices, which is added to meats and fish to both cure and flavor them.

Cure. A dry mix or brine containing salt, sugar, and other seasonings. The mixture may or may not contain curing salts.

Curing. The process of placing meat or fish into a brine or of rubbing the dry mix into the food, and letting it stand for hours or days until it is "cured." The food is then dried or smoked, or both.

Curing salts. Another name for "cure." May be a small amount of sodium nitrite and sodium nitrate on a salt carrier, or in the case of saltpeter, may be potassium nitrate or potassium nitrite.

Dehydrator. A device used to dry foods.

Dress. To clean and remove the entrails of game animals.

Dry cure. A mixture of curing ingredients without a liquid. The dry mix is rubbed onto the surface of meat and fish.

Dutch oven. A round kettle, with three short legs, a flanged lid, and a bail, frequently made of cast iron and used to cook over camp fires.

Enzymes. Any of various organic substances that are produced in plant and animal cells and that cause changes in other substances by catalytic action.

Fat back. Fat from the back of hogs, used primarily for barding.

Fillet or filet. A boneless, lean piece of meat or fish.

Fillet knife. A thin, flexible knife used for filleting fish.

Filter feeders. Shellfish that obtain their food by sucking seawater through their siphons and extracting microscopic plankton.

Firebox, fire pit, fire chamber. The area where the fire is built to smoke the food.

Freezer tape. Tape especially made for use under freezing conditions.

Game animal. Any animal that is legal to hunt for food. Large game animals include moose, elk, deer, bear, caribou, and antelope. Small game animals include rabbit, muskrat, beaver, opossum, and squirrel.

Game bird. Any wild bird that is legal to hunt.

Game meat. The meat from any wild animal, including mammals and birds, that is commonly hunted for food.

Gamy. Used to describe an overly strong flavor in game animals.

Glaze. 1) A coating applied by basting food during the last portion of cooking time. 2) The shiny coating (pellicle) that appears on meat or fish after it is air-dried.

Grinder. A mechanical device, either hand-operated or electric, used to grind foods.

Hardwoods. Generally speaking, trees such as alder, oak, birch, hickory, fruitwoods, and nutwoods. These are the preferred woods for smoking foods.

Horn. (See Stuffer).

Hot-smoking. The process of drying and smoking foods at hot temperatures, often to the point of cooking.

Injecting. Using a large, specially designed syringe to inject liquids into large pieces of meat.

Jerky. Dried meat that may or may not be cured or smoked.

Kippering. The fish is heated gradually before being hot-smoked and cooked.

Kosher salt. (Also called pickling or coarse salt.) A refined rock salt used for pickling. It does not contain magnesium carbonate and therefore does not cloud brines.

Larding. The process of inserting small strips of fat into a large piece of meat, such as a roast, by means of a larding needle. The strips of fat, called lardoons, are put into the needle, which is pushed deep into the meat. When the needle is pulled out, the strips remain in the meat.

Liqueur. A spirit, usually sweetened, that is flavored with fruits, nuts, and spices.

Liquid smoke. A liquid obtained by condensing the smoke of green hardwood.

Low-acid foods. Foods that contain very little natural acid, such as vegetables, meats, and fish.

Lox. From *lachs,* the German word for salmon. Originally, a smoked Atlantic salmon made from mildly salted fish. Today, it may be fish that has been cured with salt, sugar, and spices, and may or may not be smoked.

Marinade. A liquid mixture of a variety of ingredients in which foods are soaked for hours or days before cooking or smoking.

Monosodium glutamate (MSG). A crystalline salt used to enhance the flavor of food. It is usually made from molasses or beets, and may cause allergic reactions in some people.

Nitrate. A salt or ester of nitric acid.

Nitrite. A salt or ester of nitrous acid.

Off-set fire chamber. The firebox or fire chamber set off to the side or in front of, but still connected to, the cooking or smoking chamber of a smoker unit.

Overhauling. The process of stirring the brine and meat so that the meat is evenly brined. Or, in the case of a dry cure, the process of changing the position of the meat at certain intervals.

Parboil. To boil until partially cooked, often in preparation for roasting.

Pellicle. A thin, glassy layer or glaze that forms on the surface of brined meat when it is air-dried.

Pelt. The skin of a fur-bearing animal. Often used in reference to skin being prepared for tanning.

Pemmican. An early American Indian food made primarily of powdered or ground jerky, dried berries, and rendered animal fat.

Pickling. The process of preserving or flavoring foods by placing them in a vinegar, salt, and seasoning mixture.

Pickling salt. A pure salt containing no iodine, used for pickling, canning, and brining.

Poach. To cook a food by simmering it in a seasoned liquid.

Potassium nitrate. (See Saltpeter).

Prague Powder. A trade name for sodium nitrite and salt (Prague Powder #1), or a combination of sodium nitrate, sodium nitrite, and salt (Prague Powder #2).

Preserve. To process food a certain way, such as drying, canning, or freezing, in order to keep it for extended periods of time.

Pressure Cooker. (See Canner pressure cooker).

Propane. A colorless gas used for fuel.

Pumping. (See Injecting).

Reduce. To simmer or boil a liquid down to concentrate the flavors or thicken the liquid.

Render. To cook fat until it liquefies.

Salinometer. A device to measure the salt concentration in a solution, such as brine.

Salmonella. Bacteria that causes food poisoning, specifically, an intestinal infection.

Salt. Usually refers to sodium chloride, better known as table salt.

Saltpeter. Potassium nitrate. A white, crystalline powder that has a salty, slightly bitter taste.

Seelachs. A food made from white-fleshed ocean fish that has been treated with salt, then sliced, dyed to resemble salmon, and lightly smoked.

Shuck. To remove the shells from shellfish.

Smoke chamber. The chamber that contains the wood smoke and the food to be smoked.

Smoker. Any unit in which foods are smoked as they dry or cook.

Smoking. The process of applying smoke to food.

Smoke-cooking. A hot-smoking process in which the food is fully cooked as it is being smoked.

Sodium nitrate. A sodium-nitrogen salt used in meat cures, explosives, and fertilizers.

Sodium nitrite. An ester or salt of nitrous acid, used in curing meats.

Softwoods. Includes conifers such as firs, pines, spruces, hemlocks, and cedars. As a general rule, these woods are not used when smoking foods because they impart a too-strong, sooty, or pitch flavor.

Staphylococcus. Bacteria that produce a toxin in foods that is very resistant to heat.

Steam. To cook in a vapor over steaming or boiling liquid.

Stockinette. A casing made of loosely woven cloth or string that is pulled over large pieces of meat such as hams and turkeys before cooking.

Stockpot. A large, straight-sided pot that is taller than it is wide.

Stuffer. A tube or funnel used to transfer the ground meat and seasonings from the grinder into the casings when making sausages. Also called a horn.

Suet. The hard, crumbly fat around the loins and kidney of sheep and cattle.

Tallowy. A greasy taste or feeling.

Tenderize. To break down the tissue and fibers by marinating, curing, cooking, or pounding.

Toxins. Any of various unstable poisonous compounds produced by microorganisms and causing certain diseases.

Translucent. Permitting light to pass through. The flesh of raw fish is said to be translucent when raw, and opaque when cooked.

Trichina. A very small worm, sometimes found in pork and some game meats such as bear, which can cause trichinosis in humans when the infected meat is ingested. It causes severe illness, even death, in humans.

Trichinosis. The disease caused by the infestation of a parasitic worm called trichina.

Tularemia. An infectious disease in rodents, especially rabbits, that can be transmitted to man when handling the infected animal.

Variety meats. Includes the liver, heart, kidneys, and lungs of animals. Also called organ meats.

Water pan. A pan that is filled with water or seasoned liquid and placed on the grate above the heat source in a smoke-cooker, to provide a humid atmosphere while food is cooking.

Zest. The outer, colored portion of citrus peel, not including the white portion.

Bibliography

Aidells, Bruce, and Denis Kelly. *Hot Links & Country Flavors.* NY: Alfred A. Knopf, 1990.

Candy, Robert. *Getting the Most from Your Game and Fish.* Charlotte, VT: Garden Way Publishing, 1978.

DeLong, Deanna. *How to Dry Foods.* Tuscon, AZ: HP Books, 1979.

Eastman, Wilbur F. Jr. *The Canning, Freezing, Curing and Smoking of Meat, Fish and Game.* Charlotte, VT: Garden Way Publishing, 1975.

Editors of Consumer Guide. *Smoke Cookery.* Skokie, IL: Publications International, Ltd., 1978.

Gaida, Urban, and Martin Marchello. *Going Wild.* Sortell, MN: WATAB Marketing, 1987.

Herbst, Sharon T. *Food Lovers Companion.* Hauppauge, NY: Barron's Education Series, Inc., 1990.

Kramer, Matt, and Roger Sheppard. *Smoke Cooking.* New York: Hawthorne Books, 1967.

Kutas, Rytek. *Great Sausage Recipes & Meat Curing.* New York: Macmillan, 1987.

Kutas, Rytek. *Venison Sausage Recipes and Smoking Fish and Wildfowl.* Buffalo, NY: The Sausage Maker, Inc., 1990.

Montagne, Prosper. *Laroussée Gastronomique.* New York: Crown Publishing, Inc., 1961.

Reavis, Charles. *Home Sausage Making.* Pownal, VT: Garden Way Publishing, 1987.

Robinson, James. *The Art of Curing, Pickling and Smoking Meat and Fish.* San Jose, CA: Gordon Publishing, 1973.

Rombauer, Irma S., and Marion Rombauer Becker. *Joy of Cooking.* New York: Bobbs-Merrill Company, Inc., 1964.

Savic, I. V. *Small Scale Sausage Production.* FAO Animal and Health Product and Health Paper Ser.: 52. Rome: UNIPUB, 1986.

Stobart, Tom. *The Cook's Encyclopedia.* New York: Harper and Row Publishing, 1981.

Whelan, Jack. *Smoking Salmon and Trout.* Bowser, British Columbia: Aerie Publishing, 1982.

Index